the
best
creative
NONFICTION

Volume Volume Volume Volume Volume Volume
3

the best creative NONFICTION

Volume Volume **3** Volume Volume

EDITED BY LEE GUTKIND

W. W. NORTON & COMPANY

New York London

For information about special discounts for bulk purchases, please contact
W. W. Norton Special Sales at specialsales@wwnorton.com or 800-233-4830

Manufacturing by Courier Westford
Book design by Chris Welch
Production manager: Devon Zahn

ISBN 978-0-393-33025-0 (pbk.)

W. W. Norton & Company, Inc.
500 Fifth Avenue, New York, N.Y. 10110
www.wwnorton.com

W. W. Norton & Company Ltd.
Castle House, 75/76 Wells Street, London W1T 3QT

1 2 3 4 5 6 7 8 9 0

coordinating editors

BRUCE DOBLER

HATTIE FLETCHER

REBECCA M. GODFREY

DINTY W. MOORE

contents

Introduction: Agent of Change

Lee Gutkind

As I write this in December 2008, change is everywhere.

"Change" was the mantra of the recent presidential election, of course, the promise on which Barack Obama and Joe Biden based their campaign—and on which the McCain-Palin ticket opposed Obama. Each candidate insisted that he—and not his opponent—was the force that could shake up the status quo and turn the country around, that could bring the kind of change to heal us and unite us.

Many have compared Obama to Kennedy or Lincoln, and others speculate that his election will come to be seen as one of the most significant events in our nation's history—that what he will do next, the change he initiates, may shape the lives of many future generations.

When this book is published in the summer of 2009, Obama and his team of players will have been in office only seven or eight months, and it is entirely possible that Obama's promised "change" will not yet have materialized, or that it may have appeared in unanticipated form. (We should remember—as a former member of the previous administration pointed out in the early days of the Iraq war—that change can be messy.) Still, the nation's mood at the moment seems to welcome change—almost any change.

This volume of *The Best Creative Nonfiction* is composed mostly of work published during the past year that engages fully in the current times and provides compelling arguments for both global and individual change. Creative nonfiction's roots are in journalism, but the genre also allows writers to become intimately involved in their stories. Often this interplay between the personal and the political provides deeper coverage, and a stronger connection to the reader, than traditional journalism allows.

Wesley Yang's profile of Seung-Hui Cho, the Virginia Tech shooter, is informed by his uncomfortable sympathy for Cho, based in their common background as Asian men, aspiring writers, and, perhaps, misfits. Tim Bascom reports from his classroom in a community college in Iowa; his students' reasons for missing class, for dropping out, and for choosing their final paper topics add up to a portrait of a larger community undergoing cultural and economic transition. In "What Comes Out," Dawnelle Wilkie reports from behind the scenes at an abortion clinic—a highly politicized topic that is here stripped of the usual drama and given a fresh new look.

"Truth will always out," Wilkie writes, "and now I have spoken its name and I am waiting for the world to crumble . . ." Waiting, that is, for change.

As it happens, right now I am also going through some major changes in my life—the kinds of change many people often fantasize about and, simultaneously, resist. To begin with, I am changing jobs, leaving the University of Pittsburgh, where I have taught in the creative writing program for three decades, and where I was also an undergraduate student.

Starting this fall, I will be the writer in residence at the Consortium for Science Policy & Outcomes (CSPO) and a professor in the Hugh Downs School for Human Communication at Arizona State University. Interestingly, CSPO's mission is to consider the impact of change in a variety of disciplines. In my new position, I will help scientists, engineers, attorneys, and physicians employ creative nonfiction techniques to communicate their ideas about our changing society.

But that is only the beginning—and some of the changes I am facing seem less exciting, at least for me. My son, Sam, a high school senior, will soon be going to college somewhere and moving, perhaps, out of the house. The thought of this depresses me more than I can describe. My eighty-nine-year-old mother fears that my change in employment and location—though I have promised her I will keep my house in Pittsburgh, to maintain dual citizenship, so to speak—will keep me from seeing her on a regular basis.

But on the whole, times of change can be heady, rich in possibilities, and full of questions. What does this change mean to me and to the people with whom I have intimate connections? What will I learn about myself, about others, about the world because of these changes?

As a writer and editor, this is what interests me most about change. It is complicated, painful, and promising, and therefore rich in literary possibilities, from plot and characterization to philosophical analysis, or what creative nonfiction writers refer to as "reflection." Change—for better or worse—provides writers opportunities for contemplation, speculation, fantasy, and debate. Many of the pieces in this collection find their inspiration in intense moments of change or transition—a birth, a death, the beginning of a marriage.

Brenda Miller uses the format of a table of figures to examine herself over time—her relationships with her body, her family, her lovers. Marie Mutsuki Mockett travels to Japan for her grandmother's funeral and finds equal amounts of frustration and freedom in being

only half-Japanese—as an outsider, she is not welcome at her grandmother's cremation, but her status also makes her privy to otherwise
carefully guarded family secrets. Laura Bramon Good and her husband fight through the first year of their marriage in the thin-walled
privacy of an apartment speckled with bloodstains from the previous
tenants. The death of a favorite uncle brings home the true meaning
of exile to Edwidge Danticat.

Many of the writers in this collection work primarily in other genres,
but here they tell stories—confessions, explorations, apologies—that,
in one writer's words, "I can't imagine handing over . . . to fiction." Creative nonfiction allows for intimate and honest assessment of events,
and lets writers engage fully with the rich possibilities of change.

When I started *Creative Nonfiction*, in 1994, serious writers
were dabbling with narrative, or creative, nonfiction, but aside from
the large magazines like *The New Yorker*, *Playboy*, and *Esquire*, which
published the most distinguished writers, there were few outlets for
them. Fifteen years ago, there was no market for the kind of literary,
long-form, often experimental nonfiction that appears in this collection, and most of what you will read here would likely not have
been written. The journal helped legitimize the genre and encouraged writers who work in it.

As you will see, this collection supports writers whom most large
commercial publishers and magazines don't—writers who are experi-
menting with form and language, writers who do not receive million-
dollar contracts or outlandish promotional budgets for their books,
writers whose work appears in magazines and journals (like *Creative
Nonfiction*) dedicated to publishing thoughtful, careful, unexpected
work—not just work that will sell.

We also support bloggers, whose influence on and presence in the literary world has steadily increased even in the three years we've been doing this anthology. Bloggers often beat the best news organizations in reporting major world-shaping events, and blogs are taking over the book reviewing market, to a certain extent. And generally—this is welcome news for anyone inclined to see the death of literary culture in the age of technology—blogs are becoming more sophisticated and thoughtful, as this year's selections prove. Choosing the best blogs is always a difficult task; there are so many, and the Web is increasingly home to more and more great writing. For this volume of *The Best Creative Nonfiction*, we tried something new, and solicited nominations through our online newsletter. In a two-week period, we received nearly five hundred nominations, from which we selected the seven you'll find here.

Something else that's new in this year's collection is the inclusion of promising new student writing. Last fall, *Creative Nonfiction* and Norton held a "Program-off," a national competition that challenged creative nonfiction MFA programs to submit the best work from their best students. The prize was publication in this collection and the opportunity to give a reading in New York. The winner, from Pacific Lutheran University, was Amy Andrews, who in her essay "Cantata 147: The Final Chorale" looks back at her middle-school band teacher's suicide, trying to understand, as an adult, what then made no sense to her and her classmates.

ON THE WHOLE, this year's collection of *The Best Creative Nonfiction* is a little more serious, a little more sober, a little more earnest than in past years. Perhaps some of this tone comes from the series editors, whose choices may have reflected their own changing mood and that of the country.

And yet, there is also much cause in this collection for optimism—for hope, another great theme of the Obama campaign. If, as it seems, we are entering a new era, we will need writers to help us navigate and make sense of the shifting landscapes of business and politics and ideas. The writers whose work is collected here grapple with life, and in so doing create writing suffused with excitement, emotion, passion, and even brilliance. Their stories reflect the changing world around us and struggle to articulate its meaning. As we look forward to whatever comes next, let us hope that, among other things, this new era will be one that values ideas, reflection, meticulously crafted narrative, and the careful use of words.

acknowledgments

Thanks to the following for their help and encouragement:
- The staff at *Creative Nonfiction*—Kim Olsen, Stephen Knezovich, Maddy Lauria, and Jack Mathews
- Amy Cherry, our editor at W. W. Norton
- Andrew Blauner, our literary agent
- The hundreds of editors who nominated work from the pages of their journals, magazines, newspapers, and book lists

Finally, *Creative Nonfiction* would like to thank the Juliet Lea Hillman Simonds Foundation and the Pennsylvania Council on the Arts, whose ongoing generosity is essential to CNF's success.

the
best
creative
NONFICTION

Volume Volume Volume Volume Volume Volume

3

An Insider's Guide to
Jailhouse Cuisine: Dining In

SEAN ROWE

*"This is one of the few stories I've written for myself, about myself,"
says Sean Rowe. "That's a dangerous practice. It's dangerous
because the more personal you get in a story, the harder it is to stay
honest. Here I think I pulled it off, but at a price: I had to reveal
things I'm not proud of to get at something bigger than me."*

I like to get in fights. I like to drink and drive. I like to kick the
windows out of cop cars and talk shit to humorless magistrates. In
my spare time I enjoy harpsichord music, quiet walks in the woods,
and fine dining. Lately, though, I have been dining in, at the Wake
County Public Safety Center, also known as jail.

The Wake County Public Safety Center is a big, ugly building
in downtown Raleigh, North Carolina. On the ninth floor, where
I spent a month in solitary confinement, the windows are painted
black so that you, the law-abiding citizen, don't have to see what is
going on inside. Good for you! But this means that if you're inside,
which you aren't, we are, you can't see outside. You cannot see the

sky. You cannot see grass or trees or hot women. You can see the marquee news crawl on the Channel 11 building across the street, if you squint through a slit my friend Jamaica scraped in the paint with a contraband razor blade.

Outside, you are safe, more or less. Again, good for you; or, as we say in the big house, Fuck you, motherfucker. Inside, well . . . let's just say one is also more or less safe, but the emphasis is on less. Look at your life-insurance policy. There in the fine print on page nine, the part I bet you haven't read, you will see that your coverage evaporates the moment you step inside the pokey. But isn't safety a relative concept?

Jail is a great place to score drugs, get gang-raped, or plot a revenge killing. It's a great place to catch up on your reading or watch a Dolphins game, assuming you're willing to throw a dictionary at the three-hundred-pound mongoloid who decides it would be better to watch the Cartoon Network. Donnie Harrison, the Wake County sheriff, says there are about thirteen hundred inmates in his jail on any given day. This is teensy, even weensy, compared to L.A. County, where I have also spent time, but that is another story. A small portion of the Wake County prisoner population consists of actual, dangerous criminals. Another portion is made up of people who are psychotic. Not psychotic in some cutesy, figurative sense, but in the literal, DSM-IV, eat-your-own-vomit sense; in the let's-shiv-a-guard, let's-scream-all-night sense. Mostly, though, jail is full of people just like you and me—scratch that, like you—who have run afoul of America's goofy dope laws or stolen their pedophile stepfather's credit card and tried to split to Costa Rica or bounced a check at Wal-Mart and then gotten pulled over for running a stop sign three months later and busted on a bench warrant they didn't even know they had. These people are different from you in only one key respect: they are young, black, and poor.

But I am not here to whine about the criminal "justice" system or regale you with tall tales of life in stir. Let us dwell on a lighter subject:

jailhouse cuisine. During my latest incarceration, I had the pleasure of sharing Thanksgiving dinner with Mack (trafficking), Nate (counterfeiting), Outlaw (parole violation), and J.C. (conspiracy). By then I was out of solitary and had taken up lodgings at the jail annex on the edge of town. Imagine a sparkling-new airport terminal where your plane never lands or departs.

There we are, sitting at a stainless-steel picnic table bolted to the cement floor, playing dominoes, and awaiting our Thanksgiving feast, each of us wearing an orange-and-white-striped Tigger suit and matching plastic flip-flops, except for Mack, our diplomatic liaison to the black and Mexican prisoner population, who had taught himself near-fluent Spanish and ordered a do-rag ($4.10) and a pair of hipsterish high-top tennis shoes ($12.25) from the weekly commissary. J.C., whose own parents turned him in for growing a marijuana plant in his closet, is so young he has only recently started shaving. Nate is young, too, just twenty-five, but he's a hard-bitten entrepreneur who operates an auto-detailing business with his mom when he isn't printing up fake hundred-dollar bills. Mack and Outlaw, like me, are in their early forties and repeat offenders. They've been here for months awaiting trial and prison. I've already been convicted and am serving a soft jolt for drunk driving.

J.C. is giving me a crash course in Orange Cush, Skunk #7, and Great White Shark because I have decided to solve my financial problems by becoming a big-time doper when I get out of jail. Mack and Outlaw are reminiscing about chickenheads they have known. (You learn strange new words in jail, many related to sex. A "fifi," for example, is any device used as a masturbation aid behind bars; a "chickenhead" is a prostitute who services crack addicts.) Conversations in jail are not like conversations on the outside. They can go on for days, interrupted by Maury and Oprah and Jerry and Friday Night SmackDown and then resuming again, fluid, free-floating, labyrinthine. Is Rambo real? Is there really iceberg water? If not, how would you melt an iceberg and bottle it? What would you do if you won the Powerball? These sorts of questions occupy the dead hours of an inmate's life, which is to say every spare minute in between meals.

An army marches on its stomach, Napoleon wrote. So do jailbirds, though of course jailbirds don't literally march anywhere, except for Petro Sandulyak, a guy whom prosecutors described as the "godfather" of Raleigh's underground Ukrainian community. Petro ran a multimillion-dollar cleaning service that by night employed hundreds of his undocumented countrymen. His company was the principal janitorial contractor for Kmart and Kroger on the East Coast. Petro was a fat slob when I met him, but while he waited around to get convicted and pay half a million dollars in fines, serve a year in prison, and be deported, he lost sixty pounds marching in disciplined circles around the cell block. It wasn't just exercise that made Petro svelte. Diet played a big part.

Breakfast in jail is something like this: scrambled reconstituted eggs. Grits. Two slices of Wonder Bread. A half-pint of orange juice or milk. If you are like me and think breakfast is incomplete without a cigarette and a good cup of coffee, you're fucked. There isn't any coffee in jail these days and there aren't any cigarettes. That's the big difference between jail and prison; in prison—the place you go after you've been convicted of a crime or received a sentence of more than a year—tobacco and coffee, like sex, are commonly available. (In jail—the more crowded, chaotic, dangerous prelude to prison—you can buy little packets of Sanka from the Tuesday commissary, but by the time you mix instant-coffee crystals with warm sink water in an empty orange juice container you will realize it's not worth the effort. You're much better off spending your money on salt and pepper and ketchup and hot sauce, because jail food in its undoctored form is wholly unseasoned and hideously bland.) A typical lunch: spaghetti with tomato sauce. A slice each of American cheese product and cartilaginous bologna with two more pieces of Wonder Bread. A packet of cut-rate mayonnaise. Chopped iceberg lettuce and a section of unripe tomato. Iced tea (decaf). Try eating iceberg lettuce or spaghetti with a flimsy plastic spoon. For annoyance, it's right up there with showering in handcuffs.

Who assembles this slop? And where is the kitchen, anyway? When I ask Mack and Outlaw, they shake their heads at my naïveté. They know what I know now and what you're about to: that the villain of this story is LeCount Catering Services. LeCount's cost-per-inmate meal in Raleigh is $1.28. Prisoners in Raleigh don't hate the sheriff or the cops or the shaved-head, mace-toting, black-clad guards so much as they hate LeCount Catering. They fantasize about catching LeCount prep cooks in dark alleys.

You stop pooping three or four days after you're incarcerated. This is alarming until you realize that you simply aren't getting enough nutrition to create much in the way of waste. You aren't quite starving, but in the long hours of the night you think you are. The jail's operations manual states that there "shall not be more than fourteen hours between the evening meal and breakfast," and there usually isn't, but it feels like eternity. One night, Nate's snoring woke me up and I glanced over at his bunk. He wasn't snoring; his stomach was growling louder than I thought was possible for a man's stomach to growl. Some of the kindly older guards who tuck you in at night recite the following adage: "Sleep late, lose weight!" In other words: Don't under any circumstances miss breakfast.

If the low-cal diet provided by LeCount Catering Services was all there were to eat in jail, riots might rule the day. In fact, LeCount won the million-dollar jail contract in the first place because the sheriff got nervous about an uprising. In 1995, the jail quit doing its own cooking and hired Aramark Correctional Services to run the kitchen. During the next two years, complaints about moldy orange juice, spoiled milk, raw chicken, and human hair in the stroganoff went through the roof. The county commission booted Aramark and brought in LeCount Catering. Today, LeCount uses its own kitchen and trucks in the meals. No one can even remember where the old jail kitchen is located.

Jail food might be marginally better today than it was a decade ago, but thank God for the weekly commissary. Assuming you have money, and you damn sure better, you can order Cheetos and popcorn and humongous garlicky kosher dill pickles. You can order Honey Buns and MoonPies and tuna salad and peanut butter and jelly and oatmeal cookies and Pop-Tarts and chocolate pudding. You can order half a dozen kinds of candy bars, from Twix (least favorite, according to a poll I conducted) to Snickers, which outsells all other brands combined. What I haven't mentioned are ramen noodles.

Ramen noodles are a phenomenon. Because of their low cost, tastiness, and high caloric value, inmates spend upwards of half their weekly food budget on ramen noodles alone. Cajun chicken is the most popular flavor, followed by plain old chicken, beef, and chili. Last year in Houston, Texas, inmates consumed three million packages of ramen noodles. Mexican inmates save up food, including ramen noodles, and throw big late-night prayer-session picnics; black inmates trade ramen noodles for other food at regular mealtimes; white guys use crushed-up ramen noodles to make "state cakes," a sort of jailhouse pizza invented in the state prison system. Without ramen noodles, life in jail would grind to a halt.

It did in Raleigh, two days before Thanksgiving, when a memo from the sheriff appeared on the wall: effective 11/28/07 the following items will no longer be available on the commissary menu: ramen noodles.

There was no explanation for this outrage. Rumors and then conspiracy theories began spreading like Malibu wildfire: the ramen ban was an act of sadism disguised as a water-conservation measure (North Carolina this fall was in the midst of a record-setting drought); the ramen ban was an outburst of racist paranoia aimed at Black Muslims and stemming from a lamebrain muddling of the words "ramen" and "Ramadan." Finally, one night, a no-nonsense senior lieutenant of the guards appeared on the scene to clarify the situation. The ramen ban, he said, was the result of too many sinks getting clogged up by noodle flotsam, a by-product of noodle preparation, wherein hundreds of prisoners mix ramen products with hot(ish) water from the jail's sinks.

This was the grim situation that obtained on the afternoon of Thursday, November 22, as J.C. paused in his horticulture lesson and Mack and Outlaw momentarily ran out of chickenhead reveries.

Now, I know what you're thinking. You're thinking I'm going to tell you about the ghastly meal that arrived masquerading as Thanksgiving dinner, and how we subsequently set our mattresses on fire and took the guards hostage. Or you think I'm going to swipe some pampered adjectives from *Bon Appétit* or *Food & Wine* to describe the astonishing gourmet fare that LeCount Catering presented for our enjoyment—pan-seared sea scallops perhaps, with squid-ink polenta, rosemary-roasted Thumbelina carrots, and smoked salmon soubise.

Wrong.

Neither.

I'll cut to the chase, or, more accurately, the anticlimax. The trays arrived more than an hour early, at 3:45 p.m. This seemed wonderful until one sourpuss pointed out that it just meant more hours till breakfast.

What could be waiting beneath the lids of those heavy brown plastic trays? A hush fell over the cell block as a trusty lifted the first one.

Cranberry sauce, a good tablespoon or more. Sliced turkey—big, thick slices—with gravy and dressing. An actual dinner roll. Turnip greens with chopped onions. Enormous pieces of chocolate cake. Milk.

There was nothing to grouse about, and nobody did.

I LIKE WHERE liquor takes me. Usually. Selma, Alabama, might be an exception. I was minding my own business, whizzing east through the night on Route 80, halfway between my best friend's wedding in Port Gibson, Mississippi, and a nice warm bed in Savannah belonging to a beautiful witch I was dating at the time. She had promised to rub me with a secret lotion made from the blossoms of hallucinogenic flowers she grows in her tiny garden.

One part of me wished I was driving the ragtop '69 Pontiac that Rick Bragg sold me in the mid-1990s, but I owned that monstrous, smoking, fireapple-red law-enforcement magnet less than a year before my then-wife declared it was her or it. What I was actually driving was a nondescript Ford Escort with functional blinkers and taillights; and maybe just as well, since I was weaving subtly across the centerline. Good thing there's no one on the road but me, I thought, when all at once my rearview mirror erupted in flashing blue lights.

The drunk tank in Selma is downright medieval. It's a cube made out of cinder blocks with a single, billion-watt bulb in the ceiling that never goes off. Directly beneath the bulb is a hole in the floor the size of a coffee-can lid, and that's where you answer the call of nature, in front of your fellow incarcerees. There's no toilet paper or running water. There are no blankets and there's nothing to sleep on but the concrete bench running around three sides of the cell.

The thing you are never supposed to do in jail is ask another guy why he's there. Being who I am, it's the first thing I ask. "What are you in for?" I say to the guy straight across from me. After a moment of surprise he says: "Saltin'." I point to the next guy. "What about you?" He answers: "Saltin'." Twelve guys later I get to the last. "Saltin' on a officer," he says, and I finally understand what saltin' is. It's assault, and it's Saturday night in Selma.

When the sun comes up (theoretically, I mean; there aren't any windows, so I can't be sure), we hear a clanging at the big steel dungeon door. What happens next makes me think I'm still asleep, and dreaming. One by one the drunk-tank denizens get up and stagger toward the door and receive a tray through the food slot at the bottom. When I get mine, I am staring down at real, honest-to-God scrambled eggs, hot biscuits, strips of bacon, and grits pocked with chunks of melting butter. There is enough food on the tray for two men, and it is all mine. Later, at dinnertime, we get chicken sandwiches. I'm not talking about the kind of chicken sandwiches one finds at Bojangles'. I'm referring to a real Southern chicken sandwich such as you almost never see these days: two pieces of white bread with a gigantic baked chicken leg in between. A chicken leg with a goddamn bone in it. Should I describe supper? I won't. You get the idea. Next time you're arrested, do it in Selma.

When I had paid for my crimes against humanity and been released from jail in Raleigh, I walked up Hammond to Tryon and turned right, moving toward a vague recollection of a bus stop. Half a mile up the road my nose started twitching. Before me stood a faded building surrounded by cars: Larry's Southern Kitchen.

Soon I was inside noticing that the patrons divided along racial lines, half black and half white, none of them remotely skinny. The long buffet was freighted with macaroni and cheese and pinto beans and candied yams and fried trout and fried chicken and barbecued chicken and pigs' feet and gizzards-and-rice and roasted potatoes with onions; with chitlins and salmon cakes and black-eyed peas and corn bread and dinner rolls and hush puppies and country ham and fatback and grilled beef liver with onions; with biscuits and gravy, the gravy made from old-fashioned sage sausage; with chicken pastry; with pork chops; and yes, with coconut pie and pecan pie and banana cream pie and strawberry shortcake and lemon chess pie and pineapple-orange cake. I felt like a blind dog in a smokehouse, and I would still be at Larry's if it weren't for the need to make a living and get on with things. As it was, I emerged an hour later (and $8 poorer) and made my way slowly toward home through the December chill carrying a Styrofoam to-go cup of delicious sweet tea. The caffeinated kind.

Larry's Southern Kitchen does a lot of catering. I've written to Sheriff Donnie Harrison, enclosing a small check for his re-election campaign and suggesting he fire LeCount Catering and let Larry's crew take over the food service at the Wake County Public Safety Center and its sparkling new annex. Harrison's a busy man, and so far he hasn't written back.

thing she wanted. Mildred said, "You tell him he doesn't have anything I want." But she understood she was ripe, that this would be the first of many offers.

The house of prostitution was an ordinary house on an ordinary street in downtown Raleigh, North Carolina. For the purposes of the novel, I changed the setting early on to a fictionalized version of Morgantown, West Virginia. This act was essential in liberating me from the confines of factuality.

Outside of Raleigh, there was a big operation called Sugar Hill, a more factory-run institution that could handle the rushes of harvests and major conventions. But Ella's house relied on regulars. Run mainly during the years of prohibition, its business was successful largely due to liquor sales. Some of the men just came to drink and have girls sit on their laps. This was seen as a mutually beneficial service—unburdening wives of the duties of sex and keeping prostitutes away from the cars that trolled the capitol. Occasionally the police would raid, but often some cops would show up the next day, returning the liquor.

To get out of the house, Mildred married at fifteen. She had my mother at seventeen. Her marriage was brutal. My mother has told me the stories of her father, Glenn, his violent streak, and how some nights Mildred would bundle up my mother and they would run off to the nearby convent to escape him. He was a villain while drunk, but my mother has tried to explain that, when sober, he was a hero. He was both the one they were running from and the one they were waiting for to come and save them.

I realized in the long talks with Mildred and her recorded late-night whispers there were stories my mother didn't know. Every once in a while, my mother would ask what I'd learned. I was careful. I told her the story of her father baptizing his brother dying on the bathroom floor. I told her how later the uncle came to Mildred in a dream and said, "I have seen the faces of all the angels in heaven." But

Literary Murder

_____

JULIANNA BAGGOTT

Julianna Baggott, who is best known for her novels, finds both freedom and limitations in fiction: "Novels have given me necessary veils— to hide from the audience and to hide from myself," she says. "And I've found that I've learned a lot about the inner workings of human beings and my own inner workings because I could rely on those veils." In this essay from the Cincinnati Review, *about the experience of writing a novel based on her family's history, Baggott focuses on "the moment when the veil is stripped away, and the writer must 'fess up to what they've done—for better or for worse. . . . When you write a novel based on a true story as I did in* The Madam, *I think it's only fair to acknowledge—in some way—what is the deepest truth embedded within the novel, and where you've taken the greatest license."*

My grandmother still keeps the hours of the whorehouse. She stays up late at night and sleeps until noon. It's the natural clock of her childhood, and therefore, I suppose, hard to break.

When I began writing *The Madam*, a novel based on my great-grand-mother's life as a madam and my grandmother's as the daughter of one, I interviewed my grandmother in her condo's pink living room with its fringed lamps and plastic runners, an aged poodle in her lap. But because her mind is most fiery in the middle of the night, I taught her to use a handheld tape recorder when the mood struck. And I confess, this was easier for me. I sat in my office and listened to her southern lilt; and when the story bore down on me, I pushed stop.

I fell in love with her the way you fall in love with a new baby. In a strange reverse genealogy, she became my own child. And so I started writing *The Madam* in a flawed state. Instead of purity of artistic purpose, I had an ulterior motive. I wanted to resurrect the past and save her from it.

Looking back, I can only guess when I first found out about my grandmother's childhood. The youngest of four and my mother's confidante, I was kept home from school if it was too cold, too rainy, too pretty a day to stay cooped up. Did she tell me on the sunporch, in the car? While we were eating lunch or playing rounds of casino? Did she tell me before I could really understand? At nine or ten? The knowledge sank in slowly through my teens, and by college it was a story I could almost tell. It seems I've always known it.

My mother, however, didn't know until after she was married. In fact, my father told her. He put together my great-grandmother's past from loose, drawling conversations that men have among themselves on southern porches. As my parents drove away from my grand-mother's house in Raleigh, their Toronado rolling up Route 29 to their Alexandria walk-up, my father started talking about my great-grandmother, Ella, a wide-mouthed old woman who then rented rooms and sold dresses off her front porch.

At first, my mother denied it. But then she grew quiet, because it made sense. She remembered once when she was thirteen and out with Ella in downtown Raleigh, they bumped into a man her grandmother's age, and she recalled her grandmother saying, "This is my granddaughter, Glenda. She's sixteen and hasn't ever had a boyfriend." It embarrassed my mother. She was a skinny, shy girl. But my mother also recognized that some other kind of conversation was happening, something she didn't understand. It stuck with her. In the car with my father, she suddenly knew her grandmother had been telling the man that she was on the up-and-up and out of the business now.

My mother remembered, too, that not much later Ella pulled her aside in the middle of something routine—doing dishes or rolling hair—and said, "One day you'll hear things about me, and I want you to remember this: I put my children to bed hungry one night and I vowed I'd never do it again." This has become family lore, an ancestral mantra. Is it a rationale? A comfort to us, said with daring pride?

Newlyweds, my parents drove north silently, away from the South and her family. A grackle hit the windshield, then fluttered up and over the car. My father slowed instinctively, but my mother said, "Keep driving." They didn't go back to inspect the damage.

MY GRANDMOTHER, MILDRED, is the kind of woman I can call in the middle of a Tuesday afternoon and with little introduction ask, "How much for a blow job in 1931?" She'll say, "Well, now, straight sex was two dollars, and a blow job was five, and to go down on a girl—they were called Mr. Pansy—that was the most expensive at six." She'll tell the story of a kinky customer who liked to have toma-toes thrown at his rump. And the story of how she knew she would have to leave her mother's house: A man offered one of the prosti-tutes fifty dollars to arrange a date with my grandmother. She was fourteen. Knowing she was the madam's daughter, he'd approached the prostitute instead, telling her that he would give Mildred any-

I didn't tell her that her other uncle had tried to rape Mildred when she and Glenn were newlyweds, that she beat the uncle with the spike of her heel, that he ripped her dress, and that when she finally told Glenn, he laughed, saying she must have tempted him, that she must have looked too pretty in her print dress.

My mother could sense I was holding back. She said, "I don't want to know it all, do I?"

I told her no.

Again, it would have made sense to her. It would have fit in with her odd childhood memories. Other children are told not to go home with strangers. My mother was told not to go home with her uncles. "They may say I sent them to pick you up," Mildred warned, "but I would never send them. I'm the only one who will pick you up at school. If they come for you, stay put."

THE KNOWLEDGE OF my family's strange, desperate (sometimes conniving and glorious) past has undoubtedly pushed me to be a novelist. Maybe my mother's confessions primed me for storytelling. Perhaps it was the prostitution itself, a secret sprung loose, and everything that came with it that pushed me into writing. Prostitution could be a screen through which I view my entire family's history: my grandmother's agoraphobia and addiction to Valium in the '70s, her daily use of Mevacor for her nerves, her "sinking feelings," her obsession with a clean body; my mother's obsessive-compulsive disorder; even my own compulsive writing and oddities and bouts with insomnia. How far can I take it?

I've heard myself say: I believe in the hard sell of literature. And I do, because I've heard of more precious things sold for less. Unlike some high-minded writers, I have no hang-ups about marketing art, which has brought me to this: I wrote *The Madam* because I had to, for my family, but I also knew it would be a marketable idea. I'd learned to cart out the family's lurid past in interviews and Q-and-As and panels. It's what people wanted to hear: the whores, the pool-hall hustlers and snake-oil salesmen. And so aren't I guilty of whoring them out again? I'm a madam selling family, a whore of my own art. I can't go around judging.

And yet judgment was a constant threat while writing. One question swam below every conversation I had with Mildred. My great-grandmother Ella was a madam, but was she also a prostitute? The question nearly surfaced, interview after interview. And although Mildred had answered the most intimate questions about vinegar douching and Dutch caps, I couldn't imagine asking her if her mother was a whore. But I felt I had to.

One day Mildred was talking about the fact that her mother would do whatever she had to do to keep money coming in. I asked her if her mother ever ran short.

"Yes, she did."

"And did she take a date?" I'd learned to phrase it this way.

She said, "She had certain boyfriends. She would hand me a note and tell me to slip it to Mr. So-and-So behind the counter at the hardware store. I would hand the man the note, and he would give me money to take home. He was that kind of boyfriend."

Once I knew the truth, it no longer mattered. I felt myself free of it. And more important questions rose up in its absence.

Ella had three children. I have three children. I watched my children while writing *The Madam*. I stared into their faces. I kept vigil over them while they slept. I paced the house at night while their rooms filled with humidifier steam. I thought hard about what would force a woman to raise her children in a whorehouse. The question became: Do I believe the family mantra that she did it *for* her children?

I have a picture of Ella before she became a madam. It hangs on the red wall of my entranceway. She's fourteen. She's wearing a crepe-paper dress she made herself. Her thick curly hair falls wildly down

her back. Hands on her hips, she glares at the photographer. She's a
defiant girl. She will become a defiant woman.

I believe she put her children to bed hungry one night. I believe she
made an angry vow. But I don't really buy her story. Others survived
the Depression on mill wages and laundry washing. Sometimes I felt
myself disengaging from her, even turning on her, which brought
on a writerly urgency, a panic. I did the only thing I could think of. I
decided that we have the same heart, a thrumming engine, something
piston-driven. It helped that I'm lustful and strong-willed, that defiance comes easily . . . naturally, perhaps genetically. It helped most of
all that I have fiction, which enabled me to become her in some way.
And I almost succeeded in not passing judgment, but I couldn't stop
myself. She failed her daughter, not by raising her in a whorehouse,
but later, at the start of her daughter's violent marriage. And where
my great-grandmother failed, I wouldn't.

I NEVER MET my grandfather. He died shortly after my parents
were married, shortly after that early visit south, his liver failing him
at last. I know that on that visit he took my father into the back bedroom. He pulled a German Luger from the top of the closet. My
father thought he was going to shoot him. Glenn was ominous that
way. But instead the old man cradled the gun. In retrospect, he wasn't
an old man. He just looked old.

"This is for you," he said, handing the Luger to my father, who is
awkward with manly things like guns. His own father had died when
he was five, and he was raised by his mother and old maid aunt in a
house with his two sisters. He held the gun as best he could, trying
not to set it off.

My father said, "I didn't know you served in the war."

Glenn told him he hadn't, that somebody owed him money on a
bet and this was the only way the man could pay up.

It's my grandfather I'm after. He's the one I've been hunting for years. It was during Mildred's stories about him that I would push the stop button on the recorder and walk out of the room to the clatter and hum of my ordinary kitchen and stand at the sink to cool my wrists.

One day, shortly after I told my mother she didn't want to know what I was learning in those interviews, she stopped in the yard as I was leaving her house. The kids were climbing into the car.

"He wasn't perfect," my mother said. "And I will spend the rest of my life trying to forgive him. But once, when he was going through a long sober stretch, he was watering the yard with his thumb over a hose, and I told him that I'd learned this line from Shakespeare: 'And jocund day stands tiptoe on the misty mountain tops.' He repeated it. He didn't know what it meant, but he loved it. He had that capacity for appreciation."

DESPITE HER CIRCUMSTANCES, my grandmother insists that her childhood was happy. Like the timeless Hollywood tradition— hooker with a heart of gold—she claims all the prostitutes were good-natured and fun loving. A lot of them had husbands and boyfriends whom they lavished with their earnings. The men who came to drink at Ella's kitchen table more often than not gave my grandmother nickels so she could run to the movie theater to see a show. "I am a happy person, Huli. It's just who I am," she says.

The story that emerged, however, from the accumulation of details speaks of a less-than-happy youth. Ella was married five times in an era when it took five years to get a divorce. When she decided to run off with a man, as she did periodically, she put Mildred and her slightly retarded brother in the orphanage, where my grandmother would cry in the play yard while Willard petted her hand through the fence separating boys from girls. Mildred didn't go to school until third or fourth grade, because each year Ella brought her, Mildred would get in such a hysterical state, Ella would hug her to her chest and take her home. She quit school a good bit before she got married at fifteen, and there marks the official end of her childhood.

After she read *The Madam*, she said she liked it. She said it was good. Then she said, "Next time maybe you can write about the family."

While I was shopping the book to publishers, my mother said, "Make them pay you a lot of money. This is your family's blood and sweat."

And after I sold it and started talking about it in interviews, Mildred whispered to my mother, "They won't hold it against her, will they?"

"What?" my mother asked her.

"Our past."

THE NOVEL IS dedicated to my grandmother, Mildred Holderfield Smith Lane, and my great-grandmother Ella, the madam. But last March, I found myself on a panel at the Tennessee Williams Festival in New Orleans. The moderator asked if writing family stories was a balm for us, a healing. The others answered while I reflected on my ulterior motive—resurrecting my family's past to save them from it. Then I looked out into the packed audience, the crowded balcony, and I realized that I hadn't written the book for my grandmother or for my great-grandmother or for myself. I'd written it for my mother. I was saving Mildred on behalf of my mother, who'd been a little girl in a tempestuous household, who'd wanted to but couldn't.

I told the audience that my mother doesn't think of herself as articulate, but she needed to voice this story. She needed a document. And it's my mother who loves this novel. I told the audience that she tears up when she talks about it, a steam of pride in her chest that rises to her face.

And here I asked myself: Does she know I have a confession? My mother has allowed me to write about anything I want. She's fond of the story of Mrs. Faulkner confronted at a bridge party by a woman who was disgruntled that Faulkner wrote about the people in town. Mrs. Faulkner said simply, "My son writes what he has to write." Fiction is my airtight alibi. My mother would excuse any way that I manhandled truth to make art. She would say that I had to invent the novel's ending to make it more interesting.

But I didn't. I took morbid pleasure in the ending. I'm guilty.

I MURDERED MY grandfather. It was a literary murder. I raised him up, dressed him in different clothes, gave him a different name, put him in a different town, and killed him.

The first time my grandfather beat my grandmother, she got on a bus. She had her period and turned over the pad because she didn't have another one. She bled onto the back of her dress. She arrived on her mother's porch, bruised, swollen, desperate. But Ella didn't take her in. She sent her daughter back.

This is the part of the story I cannot bear, not of a girl being raised in a whorehouse, but a girl who wants to come home and is sent away. This is the part of the story I raise up from the dead. I turn it on its ugly head. A body of water, an accident, a rock, if necessary, on his skull. I write it my way. It is the fiction writer's prerogative. The madam didn't seek retribution for her daughter. She turned her head, and I had to kill him myself.

Rock Dust

STAN BADGETT

The editors of the Minnetonka Review, *where this essay appeared,
admired Stan Badgett's writing for its use of "precise and elegant
prose, a strong atmosphere, and vivid imagery to conjure for the
reader a fresh and evocative narrative." Badgett earned his prose
the hard way, by working as a miner, underground—"a raw, cold,
suffocating place"—for seven years to support his family. Still, he
says now, the experience was essential to his development as an
artist: "The coal mine broke things loose in me. It was the crucible
that turned me into a writer."*

Cold, white dust collects on mine timbers like rime frost, lies a
foot deep on the floor. You glide through it, surf through it—
the dust is soft like talcum powder. You kick it up with your feet as
you walk. Plop, plop.

Federal law requires everything in the coal mine to be covered
with pulverized limestone—it's supposed to dampen an explosion.

There are rock dust "stations" underground—yellow holding tanks buried under years of accumulated dust. You have to dig through layers of it just to find the hatch door.

Rock dusters (men on graveyard who spray the mine with dust) wrap up in burlap to stay warm while they're minding the tanks. You get chilled down if you're not wrapped up. You push a lever to pump white dust through the lines, then settle back for a twenty-minute snooze.

Four-inch aluminum pipes transport rock dust to all parts of the mine. The pipes run along the roof at skewed angles, suspended from J-hooks and baling wire. Every so often, flexible hoses hang down from shut-off valves. Here and there, little plumes of dust emanate from quaint pots and drums resembling old-fashioned stills. These are called "trickle dusters."

You wake from your nap and walk the dust lines, opening valves along the way, blasting the passageway with thick, choking clouds of white. You get dizzy, can't tell right or left, up or down. A man approaching from a few feet away—his caplight beaming right into your eyes—seems to be drifting in from another planet. The stuff frosts the insides of your nose, cakes your eyebrows and eyelashes, grits your teeth. It sifts into your boots and fills up your gloves. Sometimes you wonder how, after so many years of this, there is any room left in the tunnels at all—you'd think they'd be totally plugged up with dust. You go out the hole at 6:45 in the morning, leaving the mine pristine white. When you come in at 11:00 that night, the tunnels are coated with a fine layer of sooty black, and it's time to start over again.

Rock dust comes in ninety-pound sacks. It's ground-up limestone, calcium carbonate quarried from the walls of Glenwood Canyon. Tons of the stuff come into the mine every night on little railcars called the "trip." You off-load the sacks by hand, stacking them like sandbags around a combat trench. You work up a sweat. The dust-covered paper slips through your hands and sends a gritty chill down your backbone.

I remember bringing in a load of dust one evening and stacking the sacks. A fellow named Mark Edwards helped me. We made swift work of it, then chatted awhile. Mark stood opposite me on the other side of the stack, smiling. The next day a section of roof collapsed and killed him.

I have an indelible image of another man, Big Bird, whose real name was Mike. When I think of rock dust, I think of him. There had been a terrible gas explosion at the mine. Fifteen men died. There were union meetings and safety demands, and the men voted to go on strike. The last shift before going on strike felt unreal. Gloom hung heavily in the tunnels. I could imagine the white flash, the concussion, the melting heat, bodies strewn across the floor. At the end of the shift we rode silently out to the track, crammed into the back of a diesel-powered Scout. We didn't know when we'd return.

At the tracks we climbed onto mine cars, which were nothing more than sheets of flat steel mounted on wheels. A low guardrail of heavy pipe surrounded each car. Bags of dust were stacked on the cars four deep. As the trip lurched forward, and we began our ascent, one of the men grabbed a bag, ripped it open, scooped up several handfuls of dust, and flung them all directions.

The tension broke as one man after another grabbed a fistful of dust and pitched it at the nearest smiling face. We were eating it, wiping it out of our eyes, laughing our heads off, and Big Bird planted both feet firmly on the floor of the railcar, tore a sack in two, and heaved a good forty pounds of dust at one of the slaphappy miners, plastering him against a guardrail. It was no-holds-barred the rest of the way up the tunnel. Big Bird took some hefty shots but never went down. He just stood there unbudged, coated with white from head to foot. I can still see the wet curl of his lip, the smirk of triumph in his eyes.

Show, Don't Tell

THE EDUCATION OF ORONTE CHURM
(INSIDEHIGHERED.COM)

"The soul has no assignments," Randall Jarrell says. "It wastes its time." That's never more obvious than when you're trying to teach your five-year-old everything he needs to know about the place you grew up so that he'll become, well, you.

"Thank you, Daddy, for teaching me all these things," he says politely, trapped in his car seat by a five-point harness. "But, Daddy? Can we get hamburgers for lunch or not?"

Most know little about southern Illinois. It's at the same latitude as Richmond, Virginia, and had a strong secessionist movement, despite Grant using Cairo to control the Mississippi and Ohio rivers. (My father remembers an anvil on display in the town where he grew up that had been broken, in one of the town's anniversary celebrations of Lincoln's murder, by "shooting" it—loading gunpowder into it and blowing it sky-high. One wishes fewer had dodged it on its way back down.) The voices sound mid-southern, especially those of older people, who've distilled local speech with age.

Southern Illinoisans eat according to various cultures that worked the mines—grits, biscuits and gravy, ham steaks with gravy, fried chicken with mashed potatoes and gravy, black-eyed peas, greens, and God's own sweet corn and tomatoes; costolette, scaloppini, rolladi, lasagna, pasta verde, polenta, risotto, and crucants (most of the Italian-Americans in my town were descendants of Lombardy); the occasional white-tailed deer, quail, wild turkey, Canada goose, bluegill, and catfish; strawberries, red, black, and purple raspberries, apples, peaches, pears, blackberries, blueberries, grapes, and cherries—though not always at one sitting.

The bottom quarter of Illinois, where I'm from, is called Little Egypt. One explanation is the bounty of its orchards, fields, lakes, and rivers: One year in the nineteenth century the upper Midwest had a bad winter, then lost its crops the following summer, and it was saved by milk and honey from southern Illinois. Others say the name refers to the promised land imagined by African-Americans fleeing the Reconstruction South. Newcomer Chicago spread the rumor with her wild-onion breath that Little Egypt is a gaunt-cow- and locust-plagued wasteland.

The area is a geologic anomaly. The Pleistocene glaciers that ground down most of Illinois never arrived in southern Illinois. So while it didn't get the utterly flat yet fertile farmland of upstate, it kept its enormous sand-stone bluffs and rock formations (the odd "streets" between the building-sized rocks of Giant City State Park). Teeming with flora and fauna that in some cases look positively Jurassic, it's part Ozark Plateau, part coastal plain of an ancient inland sea. Streambeds and highway cuts are full of fossilized ammonites, corals, sponges, Archimedes screws, and trilobites, as well as the fossil ferns, grasses, and other swampy plants that sprouted and died over the Pennsylvanian Period and became bituminous coal. The local economy boomed along on that high-sulfur coal for a couple of decades, then went bust and never recovered. It hasn't been easy. The people of southern Illinois are warm and suspicious, often silent but as easily voluble, and natural storytellers. Having been away awhile, I'm the least funny one in the bunch.

I wanted Starbuck to know all this, just for context. Then we would drive past all the places of my childhood, and I would say, There, my boy—you see? across that field spotted with lightning bugs?—*there* I used to make hot-air balloons with my friend Eric out of plastic sheeting and pie plates and release them after dark. They were mistaken for UFOs, and we listened to a CB radio and giggled as drivers in the vicinity shouted and swore over the airwaves at the sight. Eric's dad was an electrician at the mines, a huge man with swollen fists, and he and his tiny wife had four big sons. The family sometimes lived on aid when Eric's dad was laid off again, but because he was a mechanical genius, they owned an airplane, dirt bikes, a dune buggy, a motorboat, and cars too exotic to identify in mid-America back then—Saabs, Peugeots, Jaguars, Porsches, and one of those with its only door in front between the headlights. It sat in the woods out back, awaiting its turn to be restored in the building they all called The Shop. Eric's dad had a heart attack in his Piper on the approach to our local airport, and his quiet tiny wife had to land the plane herself—her first time at the controls. She clipped a light pole on descent but rolled up safely with her dead husband next to her.

Problem is, I could *tell* Starbuck whatever I wanted, but he wouldn't retain it. I'm sly enough to *show* him instead. While we were in southern Illinois, I let him play with friends' kids in the city park where I learned to swim and play tennis. I walked him down several trails through sandstone bluffs, and we climbed a dry waterfall. College students had stashed empty beer bottles under a boulder at the top of the cliff, and Starbuck wanted to know if they were from, you know, not dinosaur times, maybe, but from ancient times, like back when the cowboys lived, or something. . . . Could be, I said.

He wanted to know why there was a filthy waistband ripped from a pair of underwear up there too, and I said maybe somebody had wanted to go swimming *real bad*. I could see him thinking. We hunted fossils while mosquitoes whined in our ears, and I played music too loud in the car and let him drink all the root beer he wanted on the way home. *This* is the education of Oronte Churm, which we won't reveal to Mrs. Churm, who sometimes wants to confer on my methods.

The Rope Swing, the Swastika, the Oldest Whale I Know

Scott Black

The editors of Isotope: A Journal of Literary Nature and Science Writing, *where this story first appeared, say they look for "nonfiction work that combines lyrical language and personal narrative with subjects in science and nature, which we define broadly. We look for beautiful writing that explores the complex and intimate relationships between the human and non-human worlds"—as in this piece about an afternoon spent near a waterfall.*

There was something very erotic about watching my best friend's wife piss into the river. A former lifeguard with long lithe legs, tall cheekbones, and short blond hair, Penelope sat waist-deep in a shallow pool scooped out of limestone by thousands of years of erosion. A green one-piece bathing suit clung to her contours. Concentrating, she closed her eyes, exhaled, looked up at me, smiled. I threw a twig into the water in the middle of where I judged her pee to be, watched as it was borne toward the edge of the waterfall, toward her husband and others frolicking in the pool below, toward the rope swing we had come for. I didn't know what to make of it.

I still don't, and wonder why it sticks with me, this peculiar moment. What exactly was I thinking? I'd like to know. It's different now—immediacy gone forever, replaced by imagination; by highly suspect fragments of image and threads of narrative; by a powerful but elusive emotional impression. And so I grasp at it, clumsily scattering the pieces, gathering them, fitting them together as best I can to see what takes shape.

My best friend, Sam; his wife, Penelope; and Keith—that was our merry band, all of us in our middle twenties. On the way to the rope swing, Keith and I had smoked a joint in the back of Sam's box-shaped topless CJ-7 Jeep. The Jeep's knobby tires hummed deeply against the highway, the moist hot summer wind blasted into our faces and past our ears, the THC seeped into our brains.

I have no idea where we went, other than somewhere in north-eastern Alabama, where history is everywhere on display. The brick-red clay underfoot, which turns rivers maroonish brown, is indicative of an abundance of iron oxide in the soil, and below it, too, deep in the earth, which made Birmingham a center of mining and steel production, the so-called "Pittsburgh of the South." The hills and valleys, knobs and ridges, evidence of the same seismic event that bore the ancient Appalachians, eventually flatten out south of Birmingham and ease into a floodplain with a richer, loamier soil.

This land of humid heat and hills and rusted dirt is heavily forested—70 percent of the state is covered by a combination of oak, hickory, and pine. Ninety-five percent of this land is privately owned, mostly by timber companies, industrial farms, real estate barons.

But we had not left behind the city of Huntsville and the marked roads to enter some secret haven of the gilded southern aristocracy. It was no surprise, then, that at the end of a nameless dirt road we found old American pickups parked and locked beneath a store-bought "No Trespassing" sign nailed to a pine. A trail curved into the trees.

There is an element of chance to encountering people back in the woods, far from police and hospitals. I had seen, out in the country, pointless fistfights and pocket knives drawn over too long a look, or one too many beers. I had also seen, though, simple reflexive courtesy and kindness from people who live in small towns you've never heard of, towns with names like Paint Rock, Sweet Water, Cuba, Coffee Springs, Wedowee, Boligee, Brilliant, Dodge City, Allgood.

Penelope, who grew up in Elkmont, Alabama, which holds somewhere between four and five hundred people, knew all this. She had not seen high school pep rallies erupt into gang fights that spilled out of the gymnasium and into the hallways, the lunchroom, shoes squeaking, tongues cursing, blood spattering, chairs flying. But she had seen other things. In these situations, she was both more comfortable than us city boys and more wary.

On that day, though, there would be no real trouble. In that boundless pagan cathedral filled with butterflies and horseflies, rattlesnakes and hummingbirds, greens and browns and yellows in the woods and wispy whites far up above against the fierce cobalt sky, trouble seemed very far away.

We clambered out of the tall jeep, grabbed towels and cigarettes and plastic bottles of soda, and filed into the forest down the path, which looked to double as a streambed during heavy rains. Keith lit another joint and inhaled and passed it to me and I sucked in the pungent smoke and let it linger in my lungs. Sam and Penelope, who had 9–5 jobs with drug tests, did not partake, just sauntered tolerantly along ahead of us.

We heard the place before we saw it. The first noises were faint, indistinct, and though they sounded human we could not be sure they were not the cries of birds. As we continued on, however, they became human and happy, took on gender, and we realized that all along they had been followed by a deeper sound, the sound of a large thing—like a body—splashing into water. Closer still, we heard the even lower sound of water falling from a height onto water.

Emerging from the forest into the natural clearing carved by moving liquid, we saw a muddy river, a ten-foot waterfall, and, let's say, eight people in and around the water. Rivers: future canyons, and history in the strata of even the smallest. There, on the bank, on the upriver side of trees and tangled in roots and brush high above the waterline, were collections of leaves and twigs showing where the water once had been. Further down: striated layers of mud and clay met the water, red and brown and black streaks that might one day be a piece of sandstone in the sock drawer of some earnest youth.

Beneath the sand and beneath the water was limestone, gray and chalky, porous and soft. Unlike igneous rock, which is formed when magma cools rapidly, or metamorphic rock, which is literally transformed by the tremendous pressures within the earth, sedimentary rock is formed on the earth's surface by, as you might guess, the accretion of sediment. The stone beneath was once organic material composed of vast numbers of aquatic invertebrates, which floated through the briny deep millions of years before we came sauntering down to find a rope swing Sam's cousin had told him about.

Limestone held the forest, girded the river. The place below the falls must have been especially soft to be worn away so dramatically, to leave behind such a deep, wide pool. As the water tumbled over the lip of the falls, this, too, was being slowly worn away; the lip was gradually retreating, elongating the pool below.

Limestone is composed, occasionally, too, of vertebrates. It holds fossils well. The state fossil of Alabama—who knew there were such things?—is *Basilosaurus cetoides. Basilosaurus*, meaning "regal lizard," suggests a dinosaur, but *cetoides* comes from Cetacea, the order of dolphins, porpoises, and whales. Initially misidentified, the creature was actually a mammal, one of the earliest known whales: a hairy, air-breathing, young-nursing slinky creature eighty feet long with a serpentine body and a mouth like a crocodile. Of course, we can only speculate about the behavior of the creature—whether, like the dolphin, it engaged in recreational sex—and what it actually looked like. Doubtless the drawings we see, based on what we know of its skeletal system and the anatomies of other whales, are pretty accurate, but in the end they still represent the vision of the artist.

Five teenagers were down below the waterfall—two young women sitting on the bank in shorts and bikini tops, one shirtless young man sitting beside them and smoking a cigarette, one shirtless young man standing next to the tree the rope swing was tied to, and one shirtless muscular tattooed young man flying through the air on the rope.

Because limestone is porous, streams like this one can wear holes and caves through it like bacteria through Swiss cheese. Spelunking is big in northern Alabama. You can slip into interconnected networks of caves looking for adventure, see tiny bats, step in huge mounds of their guano, shine light on albino catfish that can't see it, wriggle through foot-high spaces behind your best friend's mom, whose muddy butt blocks the light from her headlamp but shines darkly in yours. You can get lost if you're not careful. Before you, thousands of years before, people lived in these places. One particular cave, Russell Cave, near Bridgeport, Alabama, has been occupied for thousands of years by different tribes of peoples. Following a joint study of the cave by the Smithsonian Institution and the National Geographic Society in the '60s, the NGS purchased the cave and donated it to the nation. It is now a U.S. national monument. What began long before nations and states will continue long after. Do you remember water on Mars?

We walked upstream, where a sunburnt middle-aged couple was splashing with a little blond girl in the shallows at the beveled edges of the river, and found a place to put our things. We said hello, took off our shirts and shoes, piled them on a rock next to our towels, and walked in the tepid river up to the edge of the waterfall. We looked down to where the water was crashing into the pool, bubbling and roiling. It looked higher from up there, and we weren't sure what sharp branches poked up from below the water's surface, so we watched awhile as the guys went off the swing, forming mental maps of the safe zone in the center of the pool.

Excavation is risky—one can mistake mammal for reptile, fit together bones from entirely different creatures (intentionally or not), and produce the remains of something that never existed. This happened in the 1840s, when a leviathan was assembled from the bones of various animals, including *Basilosaurus*. The man who concocted it toured the United States and Europe, charging admission to his exhibit of "sea serpent" skeletons.

The group below watched us watch them. "Jump in," they called at last, knowing we wanted to. And so we did. Keith went first, yelling as he fell and curling into a cannonball; then Sam, silently windmilling his arms until the moment he splashed down; then I jumped forward and grabbed a breath before kerplunking into the water and hearing the bizarre splooshing sounds beneath it. When I came up, I swam toward the swing, following Keith and Sam. Climbing out, I noticed that the bottom was rocky, but felt no dangerous tree branches. Penelope was walking down on the trail beside the waterfall. She didn't mind water, but was afraid of heights.

We talked awhile to the people. Or Keith and Sam and Penelope did. I was—and am—shy, timid, awkward, and aloof around strangers. I climbed the makeshift ladder on the side of the tree—slats of wood nailed into its trunk—caught the rope Sam swung in my direction, took a deep breath, tightened my grip just above the knot on the coarse thick yellow rope, pushed off the tree, and arced down and then up, aiming for safety. Adrenaline and THC boiled through my synapses. At the apex of my swing, I kicked my legs up and let go of the rope, spinning up into the air, weightless, exalting in the vertigo, turning a backflip and landing with a splash in the center of the pool. Kerplunk. Sploosh. They were all smiling when I surfaced, and I tried not to. "Nice," said the guy with the tats, and I nodded. I waited my turn, did it again, then followed Penelope back up the trail for a cigarette.

My relationship with Sam's wife had followed a strange trajectory. At first, I was fiercely against her. This was in large part due to my being jealous at her cutting into our friendship, making him want to get a steady job in our hometown and opt out of the grand adventure we had planned in Alaska. There was also her country way of think-ing, which seemed to me silly and superstitious. And then there was her temper—for all her sweetness, she could turn fierce and furious. She's "high strung," he admitted first, and then later "she's a wild-cat." So there was that. Later, though, we grew closer, and talked, and developed that strange bond women and men who would not normally associate can grow into when thrust by circumstance into platonic interaction. She thought me handsome and sweet, told me I would someday make some woman very happy. And was there not a certain spark at times when we laughed?

One time, we dared each other to eat a piece of dried dog food—a man and a married woman, both, presumably, adults, sitting in her front yard while her husband turned wrenches beneath his jeep—and I had gone first, then made a face when she popped hers in her mouth and started crunching. She had giggled and slapped my shoulder and crunched down again and he had slid out from under the vehicle and said, "What are you guys doing?" The look we exchanged had been just slightly guilty. Not guilty in the way we would have been if plan-ning a tryst, or even sneaking a peck under mistletoe, but just mildly guilty as though we had inadvertently crossed some spiderweb-thin line by having too much fun there without him, by forgetting, for that instant, that he was there.

We walked back up to our things and lit cigarettes. Penelope sat down in a shallow pool near the riverbank and I sprawled beside her on a rock. We both just sat there silently for a moment, lolling, hearing the water, smelling the clay, feeling the cool wind and hot sun on our wet skin, blowing beautiful streams of cancer into the air and seeing them fade to nothing, watching water spiders supported by surface tension skate nimbly around and across the river's skin.

Aldous Huxley, in *The Doors of Perception*, wrote about taking mescaline. The title comes from a William Blake quote: "If the doors of perception were cleansed every thing would appear to man as it is, infinite." In this writing, Huxley—working with ideas from "the eminent Cambridge philosopher, Dr. C. D. Broad"—proposes that the human brain is essentially a "reducing valve," the function of which is to winnow down and order vast quantities of information, to make manageable the infinite.

Every second, nerve endings all over our bodies—in our eyes, ears, mouths, noses, insides, and on every piece of our skin—are recording and streaming innumerable hordes of data. And this is with our relatively limited senses. What if we could smell like dogs, see like spiders, echo-locate like bats, read pheromones in the wind from miles away? We apprehend the world through a pinhole, and still this produces far too much information to make any sort of intellectual sense out of.

Down below, the guys continued to climb the tree and swing on the rope and drop down into the warm reddish-brown water. The girls in bikini tops still sat watching, and I wondered if Penelope was watching Sam to see if he was looking at them. I had. When we were down there, I had glimpsed the dark outline of an areola, looked quickly away, then back again. Next I observed the guy with the muscles, the sinewy flesh moving all together effortlessly, wondered what Penelope thought about that. He was sexy, hard, and glistening with water, lateral muscles taut as he hung on the rope and swung through the air.

Some say our bodies are simply DNA receptacles—ornate, graced with whistles and bells, but gene cases still. Others say that we—the squat and lithe, young and old, taut and droopy—are mere water-sacks. This is sure: water cycles through the world, floating in the air; waxing and waning in the sea; streaming, coursing, and running in rivulets across the land. It flows through plants and soil and rock, giving life and chipping slowly away at continents. It courses through our bodies, bearing plasma, working with salt to conduct electricity from neuron to neuron, toe to brain. It flushes our wastes, products of millions of biochemical reactions all working in concert to allow us to dance, perform surgery, hike, and swim.

I noticed something disturbing. The muscular guy, the friendly one who had commended my backflip, had a swastika tattooed to his shoulder. I have a friend who grew up in Cullman, Alabama, where people used to spray-paint a message on the Welcome to Cullman sign: "Niggers—don't let the sun set on your backs." These people are terrible, my friend says. They hate everyone—gay people, black people, people of different religions, people who come from other places. Yankees who talk funny. But he is these people, too, in some inescapable way. He loves his father, the Republican Southern Baptist, the mechanic, the man who couldn't bring himself to shoot his sick old favorite dog and cried when his son did.

The guy with the swastika—I was sad for him, for his ignorant, tiny world, his pinhole half-obscured. I think now of Howard Zinn revealing how the poor and dispossessed—slaves, Native Americans, indentured servants—banded together in the early days of American Colonialism, regardless of body type or melanin level, or name for the Un-nameable; of how the feudal lords had used the myth of "race" to divide and oppress.

I was also furious in a cold, bitter, pitiless way. I had grown up on army bases, become friends with people of all genetic combinations. Most of them were being threatened and assaulted by this beautiful

rune from pagan antiquity that originally symbolized the four pow-
ers of nature.

There are always people, aren't there, who know better and stand
up and say so? Buddha. Jesus. Mark Twain. Gandhi. Not me. I didn't
renounce him, or try to drown him, or talk to him about Reconstruction and the Southern underclass. I sat there smoking my cigarette
in the sun and imagined him breaking his back on a boulder hidden
below the water's surface.

Then I felt guilty, scared. What if it came true? Would Penelope
and I, former lifeguards both, feel compelled to rush down and stabilize his spine, give him CPR? What would Jesus do, indeed. I looked
over at Penelope to see if she had noticed any of this.

I have to pee, she told me.

Go 'head, said I. *What's stopping you.*

She laughed just a little

I'm peeing, she said, and I felt neurons firing throughout my
crotch, blood rushing, an involuntary spasm of my pubococcygeus
muscle.

When we speak properly of the sublime, we refer not necessarily
to beauty, but to an experience of vast power, to that which dwarfs
us, perhaps that which will annihilate us. It can be mesmerizing,
transcendental. English huddled beneath the Nazi blitzkrieg have
reported such feelings. Is this why people run with the bulls? Imagine looking up from a frail lifeboat at a hundred-foot sea, a water
wall carrying within it whole ecosystems, perhaps a *Basilosaurus*, just
before it curls and comes thundering down—with the terror, the
numbness, the sur-reality, the acute knowledge of your own mortal-
ity, would there be a deep harmonious serenity? Would it be the best
moment of your life?

She peed into the river, and I enjoyed watching. I threw a twig in
the water to escort her urine, and we watched them advance toward
the lip of the waterfall. Down below were all the people splashing

around, treading water, sitting on the bank. I kept waiting for something dramatic to happen.

What if, at the moment the twig struck the water, just before it was
driven underwater by the force of the water above it, the whole crik
turned to pee, a dirty yellow river of piss that frothed and foamed as
it tumbled into the swimming hole? What would the people do? How
about blood? What then? What might happen?

Nothing happened.

It is too much to take, the river, the forest, the world, the plan-
ets, the shimmery stars in our ever-expanding cosmos hurtling at
unfathomable speeds toward the outer edges of infinity. The world
is enough. Too much. And yet, though it sounds selfish, I sometimes
still want more.

Table of Figures

BRENDA MILLER

Teaching jobs are often seen as an impediment to getting writing done, but sometimes, as Brenda Miller discovered while writing this essay, even teachers can benefit from classroom writing exercises. "We were studying what I've termed the 'hermit crab' essay: an essay that 'inhabits' an alien form in order to deal with difficult material," she explains. "I almost didn't do the exercise (I had done it many times before), but decided to scribble for a few minutes just to see what might come up. As soon as I chose a 'table of figures' as the form, the content arrived on its own." The resulting essay appeared in Gulf Coast.

Figure 1.1: A girl becomes aware of herself as a girl. She is approximately five years old (maybe six, at the oldest seven). Note the mother instructing this girl that she must now wear a T-shirt while playing in the summertime with the boys on the block. Note the girl's naked torso, her downward gaze onto an expanse of bare flesh punctuated by two flat nipples. Outside the sun bears down, its heat insistent, but the afternoon breeze a familiar pleasure on this skin. Radiating lines from the girl's face indicate a new source of heat: the first inklings of shame. But also—beneath, within, around that shame—something more complex, a deeper pleasure, the first inklings of power.

Figure 2.3: A girl, circa age ten, lying facedown on her bed. The chenille bedspread impresses little dots on her face, her bare arms. Note how she has instinctually scooched down to the edge of the mattress, her legs straddling the hard corner. She gives a little sigh, a sigh that's almost a sob, as her body tingles all over, gives way. No one is watching, and yet she feels watched in a way that induces both shame and pleasure, the two distinctly entwined. Note the closed door of the bedroom, the absence of any adults, the room an incandescent secret, a sanctuary.

Figure 3.5: A girl, age twelve, on the diving board of her family's doughboy swimming pool. The two flat bands on her torso indicate that a bikini (polka-dotted) is being worn. Radiating lines from her torso indicate that this girl has just realized she is really, really, really in love with her belly button (a classic "inny," round and symmetrical as a dime).

Figure 3.6: Note the jutting hip bones. The high cheekbones. Collarbone swooping to her shoulders. Eyes, almost too large for her face. These, she hopes, are the beginnings of beauty, though boys sometimes still bark at her (actually bark!) when she enters a classroom. *What a dog*, they snicker behind their hands. She keeps her head up, her chin jutted out, her gaze insistently forward, though tears smart in the corners of her eyes. Acne blares on her cheeks and her chin, furious red cysts, a smattering of whiteheads across her nose. Her hair, only an hour into the day, already an oily smear across her forehead. Braces, glasses: the whole catastrophe. *A dog*. She had a dog named Sheba, a Great Dane, her coat sleek and brindled, the most beautiful creature on the planet. The boys whimper and yowl until the teacher, exasperated, finally tells them to *shut up*. The teacher says nothing to her, keeps his gaze turned away. No one, not even the girls who eat lunch with her on the playground, will meet her eye.

Figure 3.8: At home, she feels herself growing, a tingling pressure that actually stings in her bones. *Look*, she whispers to herself in the mirror, *look*. She touches these points of her body, one by one. Clavicle, Hip Bone, Lips, Eyes. Loving them. *Look at me*, she whispers. She takes off her shirt, holds her palms against the swellings of breast. This is what makes her a girl. That, and something else she can't quite put her finger on.

Table 4: Indicates the ratio of the number of fights girl has with her father, ranging from the clothing she wears (example: sheer halter top that barely covers her breasts, forcing her father to utter the word "nipple" with such embarrassed force that it startles her for a moment from her blasé teenaged countenance) to the number of boys she has kissed. Note steep rise circa age fifteen, when girl loses her virginity.

Figure 4.1: Girl lying on her bed, considering the phrase "lost her virginity." The word "lost" floats around her belly button. And she wonders how something can feel so lost when it never felt as though it fully belonged to her in the first place. She wonders how something so momentous could happen at three o'clock in the afternoon, in the full light of day, the backyard still so much itself: the jungle gym still creaking, eucalyptus trees forever shedding their bark. It took less time than watching an after-school special. *Lost. Virginity*. She wonders if there might be a lost-and-found somewhere far into her future where such things—virginity, power, self-confidence—can be reclaimed.

Plate 5: Photo of girl at her sweet-sixteen party, just days after losing her virginity. Her mother has made her a birthday cake in the shape of a green-and-white panda. Her hair is long and curls fetchingly around her face. She is smiling, indicating with one hand (like a game-show hostess) the innocent and elaborate cake. She wears a short-sleeved turtleneck sweater, green too, like her eyes. Her cheeks are unblemished, covered by Maybelline. She looks sweet. She looks sixteen. The boy to whom she's given her virginity, *lost* her virginity, hovers somewhere outside the frame, one arm around his girlfriend's waist. He holds her virginity carelessly, tossing it in one hand, like a dime-store bauble meant to last only a day. The cake glows with a gob of light that's about to be extinguished.

Figure 6.1: Girl in bed with a man. The man is twenty years old and should know better. Angry zigzag lines around the bed indicate that the phone has just rung, the father looking for his seventeen-year-old daughter, the ring of the telephone as strident as his voice will be when the man hands her the phone. *Get home right now, young lady*, his words right out of a television sit-com, her reaction scripted, too, *okay, okay*, as she pulls back the cover, slips on her jeans. She is secretly pleased to have been caught; it means she is beautiful. It means they have risked something to be together, and so she must be valuable, worth something. On her belly is an image of the man's hand, a ghostly white, each stubby finger outlined—an emblem of their day on the Santa Monica beach, his hand shading just that part of her belly, while the rest of her burned to a russet glow. She hadn't wanted to move from under his hand, to wake him, so now her skin burns under the waistband of her jeans. But his hand is still on her (fingers deftly framing the belly button) and will remain a badge of her desirability for a week. Until it fades away, the skin around this temporary tattoo peeling and singed.

Line Graph 8: The girl becomes (officially) a woman, and on this graph one can plot how her lovers accumulate. Line 1 spikes upward (number of lovers) but, surprisingly, line 2 (the sense of herself as a lovable creature) declines in parallel proportions. Line 3 (the loneliness factor) remains nearly constant. Experts call this phenomenon "Aphrodite's Paradox." Attempts to reverse this trend have thus far failed, but experiments are ongoing.

Sidebar: Clarification of Terms: She is not a *slut*, as a slut would be a woman who sleeps with anyone. A woman who *puts out*. A slut looks like a slut, whereas this woman, for the most part, dresses rather primly, in clothes that disguise her thick waist, in colors that flatter her pretty eyes, those high cheekbones. She is not *promiscuous*, exactly, as a *promiscuous* woman "chooses carelessly or without discrimination." She chooses quite carefully, dating men who are dangerously handsome, whose eyes, when focused on her, make her feel approved of by God. And when their gazes drift and falter, as they inevitably do, she feels banished, exiled from that celestial kingdom. She is *monogamous*. Perhaps she engages in what is called *serial monogamy*. In fact, she does not *date* so much as find herself in *long-term relationships* that tend to flaunt their failings quite early on, but that keep reviving *on-again, off-again*, so that her young womanhood is taken up with this exhausting dance between extremes. She'll do almost anything to make a relationship linger—cook elaborate dinners, buy sexier shoes, keep nodding sympathetically to whatever he says—terrified of being *lost*. In between these long-term relationships, she can easily go three or four years before sleeping with someone again, and during these times can convince herself she will be *single* forever and makes purchases with this prophecy in mind:

a small bed, a possessive cat, a house large enough for one. She has never borne the designations *fiancée*, *bride*, *wife*, *mother*. She is an *aunt*. She is called *auntie* by children who don't know her very well, the diminutive cute and unthreatening. She has considered the term *nun*. She mulls on the word *virgin*, how so often it means *unspoiled*. She tries not to dwell on this word: *spinster*.

Diagram 9: A schematic that shows how to use Match.com (and its parallel counterparts: Green Singles, J-Date, e-Harmony, etc.) for maximum effectiveness. "It's a numbers game," one aspirant has put it. Learn how to spot the red flags as they pop up and frantically wave. Be aware that those who have the most idealistic vision of a relationship will be those least ready for a relationship. Learn how to answer the question, asked within the first five minutes of a coffee date, "So why haven't you ever been married?" with a flippant, "I guess I've just been lucky" rather than with the retort that burns on your tongue: *I don't know, I guess because I'm just basically an unlovable person. Is that a problem?* Be aware that those who say "inner beauty" is most important will be those who, after seeing only a picture, send quick e-mails saying: "You seem like a very nice person, but I just don't sense the chemistry, the spark." Learn to distrust chemistry and sparks. Amateur chemists love to make things explode. Sparks are wild and uncontrollable; they ignite small brush fires that, even when squelched, can smolder for months.

Figure 9: A woman in bed with a handsome and sexy man. Note a mirror version of this woman hovering near the ceiling, looking down on herself in bed with a handsome and sexy man. Experts call it "disassociation"; she calls it "look-I'm-in-bed-with-a-handsome-and-sexy-man-who-wants-me" syndrome. She wonders to whom she is declaring this rather obvious proclamation and realizes, with a twinge, that she is still talking to those boys in the seventh grade, the ones who called her *a dog* and panted with their tongues hanging out. She wishes she could just stay in bed with the man, the two of them alone, without anyone watching, but knows that such a thing is impossible. Someone is always watching. Someone is always passing judgment, thumbs up or thumbs down. Thumbs press into her body all over, pointing this way and that, leaving ghostly imprints behind.

Figure 10: A woman alone in her house. She is forty-seven years old and still—after all this time—really, really, really in love with her belly button. And with her cheekbones, her clavicle, her hips. She does not love the circumference of her thighs. She still gets pimples on her chin and feels like a seventeen-year-old girl, bumbling her way into the future with a body that always betrays her, keeps aching for a specific man long after the man has departed. She's thinking about getting a dog, something mutt-like and goofy, who will adore her without reason.

She looks around her, at the couples holding hands on the board-walk, and knows there must have been some relationship manual handed out on a day she was absent. That is why she now works hard to be as present as possible. There is a Buddhist sutra she loves to read—*The Discourse on Knowing the Better Way to Live Alone*—and she always approaches it eagerly, thinking the Buddha really did fashion himself an ancient-day Dr. Phil, handing out self-help advice for the lonely and the dispossessed. And always she's surprised, but not necessarily disappointed, when the sutra says nothing about living alone; rather it instructs, in typical Socratic fashion, on how to dwell only in the present moment, unburdened by craving or regret. *Death comes unexpectedly*, the sutra whispers as an aside. *How can we bargain with it?*

Sometimes now, in the dark of her one-person bedroom, she whispers *I love you*, and kisses with her tongue the exact center of her palm, the webbed skin between her fingers. When she catches herself doing this, she feels ashamed and stops it immediately. She flings her hand away and flops over to clutch the full-length pillow that impersonates a lover under the covers. But sometimes she doesn't care, she just keeps saying it—*I love you*—and for a little while she's ushered into the lost-and-found, where she rummages through a box, sifts through those things she thought were irrecoverable: virginity, power, self-confidence. And there, too, a little rumpled but still recognizable: the T-shirt she flung off as a child, and her own small self, unabashed, chest bared in the suburban heat. And look: there's the sheath of her body, unspoiled, radiant as the day she was born.

Okahandja Lessons

EMILY RAPP

Emily Rapp finds nonfiction to be the most intimate of genres: "If a novelist invites a reader to the 'planet' or world of their story," she says, "then the nonfiction writer invites the reader into the home— into the living room, the dining room, and yes, sometimes even the bedroom. The joys of working in this slippery, always-evolving genre are an ability to create intimacy for a reader, to invite one person inside the mind and heart of another." In this essay from the Bellevue Literary Review, *Rapp struggles with how much of herself to reveal, both physically and otherwise.*

Welcome to Namibia! The battered wooden sign stood at the edge of a highway that was strewn with piles of twisted, smoking metal.

"Car accidents!" Pastor Cliff shouted above the wind and dirt spinning inside our van, which had evidently lost, or never had, glass windows.

"What about them?" I shouted back.

"The number one cause of death in Namibia!"

There were no bodies on the highway and no emergency vehicles, but the accidents appeared every few feet: grotesque, abandoned arrangements of rubber and steel, smoldering into the sky. They protruded from the land like medieval gargoyles, casting strange, tortured shadows before disappearing in the cloud of dust created by the wheels of our car. I wondered where the passengers in these burned out vehicles had ended up post-accident. Had they fled the scene? Did any lose a limb? A life?

I tugged my skirt over the hydraulic knee of my prosthetic limb to keep out the flying gravel. The inside of the leg's silicone socket was stinking and sticky from the long plane ride. I could feel an itchy rash forming on my stump, and I was anxious to get to Okahandja, to the cabin where I'd be sleeping, so that I could apply my anti-fungal cream. I'd packed all the necessary leg provisions: an extra socket in case the strap on this one broke; antibacterial soap to clean the socket; extra cosmetic hose to cover the outside of the leg when the one I wore became dirty from wearing sandals on the dusty roads.

There were no reflections on the gravel road as we sped along in Pastor Cliff's van; there were no lights except the dim blue ones illuminating the dashboard, and the headlights. I put my hand out the window and felt the air resist the skin on my arm as the van barreled into a buoyant darkness. It was unsettling to feel a part of everything: the air that smelled of burning rubber and body odor; the sound of the decrepit motor grinding into the sky; the occasional bellow of thunder far away.

There was no horizon. The stars were points of light that looked close enough to pierce an outstretched hand. The land was so dark and felt so private that the stroke of the headlights seemed unwelcome, a violation. I had come to Namibia to attend a ten-day conference designed to provide theological reflection, direction, and instruction for youth in southwest Africa, but I had my doubts; I knew a bit about the situation for disabled people in African countries. I worried this would not be an easy place to visit.

I was not prepared for this wide, black-hot emptiness. Nothing sliced up the space to make it manageable: no train tracks, truck stops, billboards, streetlights, mileage signs, rest stops, or pit stops. I was used to roads in Wyoming that climbed thousands of feet, curves buffered by mountains. In Geneva, where I'd been living in the year after graduating college, I was surrounded by manicured parks and mountain views. I strolled along cobblestone streets dotted with outdoor cafés and lined with luxury shops like Rolex and Cartier.

I'd spent most of the seven-hour plane ride from Frankfurt today listening to a repertoire of guttural pub songs performed by a group of inebriated Austrian poachers. They wore leather necklaces with white tusks that rested on the thick carpets of chest hair bursting from their open-collared shirts. One of them stumbled around in the smoking section, where I was unfortunately seated, leaving behind the scent of alcohol and cigarette smoke on his hourly visit to the toilet. "Sexy you!" he said to me as he hung on to the back of my seat, practically dragging himself up the aisle.

We landed at midnight on a strip of tar lined with weak streetlights. Inside, the airport was dimly lit and muggy. A man seated at a card table stamped my passport. At first I thought the loud buzzing noise came from the overhead ceiling lights, but I realized quickly that the noise came from the chorus of mosquitoes feasting on my arms.

Pastor Cliff, a portly, balding man, stood outside the airport entrance. His white T-shirt was patterned with sweat. His frayed cotton shorts fell just above his dusty knees, and his skin was a deep, rich black. Alone in the entrance hall, he held a sign that read MS. RATT. When we left the airport in his sixteen-passenger van, which appeared to have had some of its roof clawed off, we drove past the closed-up shops that lined the colonial streets of Windhoek. At a stoplight I looked out to the door of a shuttered store on the deserted main street. The white-skinned mannequins were illuminated by the lights of our car. Suddenly, the shop door seemed to move, and a shadow detached itself from the doorway. I jumped.

"The homeless," Pastor Cliff explained. "They're a problem here."

I watched the asymmetrical shadow hop further out into the street. It was an elderly man, an amputee. His left foot was bare, and the fabric of his right pant leg pooled on the ground. He regarded us with a mixture of suspicion and hope, and then hopped back into the doorway, his body once again absorbed in shadow.

"Many of them are damaged," Pastor Cliff said as the light turned green and we continued down the empty street.

"Oh," I said, and nodded.

A year earlier, I had stood for over an hour in a long line at the Cheyenne, Wyoming, DMV to renew my driver's license. On the back wall was a poster advertising the dangers of drunk driving. Under the familiar warning "Don't Drink and Drive" was a photograph of an amputee, the figure balanced on crutches with one pant leg pinned up to his thigh. I wondered how that man had lost his leg. I wondered how I was supposed to feel, sitting in this van now or standing in that line then, knowing I would be asked to tell my story (no, not a drunk driving accident), knowing I would have to prove that I could drive, as if I had just turned sixteen.

Now, as Pastor Cliff and I pulled back onto the gravel road in Okahandja, I thought of that young driving instructor who had asked me to drive around the block in my car. He had kept his eyes on my left leg. "Wow," he kept saying. I said nothing.

"How far does it go up?" he asked at a stoplight, staring at my lap. I didn't answer. "Shy, I guess," he said, then instructed me to "turn right when it was safe" and drive back to the DMV.

After he signed off on my license, reminding me that I was not allowed, by law, to drive a stick shift, and that I should never drive with my leg off, I drove home, shaking and silenced. Afraid to open my mouth.

WHEN WE ARRIVED in Okahandja, I settled into the bunk in my cabin, which I shared with seven women from different parts of Africa. Our days were filled with Bible studies, discussion groups, AIDS education, and teacher training for those women interested in becoming theological educators in their respective regions. I quickly adjusted to the daily routine.

Each morning in Okahandja began the same way: I woke to the sound of flip-flops on concrete, dreaming of a strong espresso. I was greeted instead with the burning-paper smell of bugs' wings in the sunlight, the smell of the salt from my forehead and neck mixed with the strange human odor of other people's bodies, the smell of warmed dirt. The gaps between the logs of the wooden cabin were intended to let in fresh air, but they served only to let in bugs.

As I did each morning, I quickly put on my artificial leg, checking first in the hollow socket area for any winged or legged creatures that might have strayed in. I grabbed my thick glasses and hobbled out to the bathroom.

The sink and shower area was packed with African women who smiled and acknowledged me when I came in, though they continued to speak in a language I did not understand. During the day, I heard the meaning of their words via the two translators, who spoke to us in their French-accented English through the headphones that everybody wore.

All of the women were naked, and their bodies were lush, full, and different shades of black. I always wore pants, a bra, and a T-shirt. I slipped my head under the brownish water that came from one of the taps. I disinfected my hands with the special soap I'd brought from Geneva and slipped contact lenses into my eyes, which were exceptionally dry and tired in Africa. I tried to look at myself—a conglomeration of shades of insipid white in the bathroom mirror. Without makeup, I had no eyelashes and my face was as pale as the moon. *You are so ugly*, is what I thought. *You are so ugly compared to all of these people.* Here were women who had come from situations of hardship and struggle that were unimaginable to me, a woman from the United States. Here I stood, with all of my privilege, envying their bodies.

I felt that my body, with its damage, marked me with shame. And even more shameful was the thought that came to me on those mornings: that I would gladly trade my body for theirs, but wanted nothing to do with the difficult circumstances of their lives.

I showered at night, when everyone else had gone to bed. I tried to ignore the enormous insects flitting in the light of the flashlight that cast my asymmetrical shadow on the stone walls. I thought of the man in the doorway in Windhoek; I thought of the poster on the wall of the DMV. I could find no right place inside my skin.

ONE AFTERNOON, HALFWAY into my trip, Pastor Cliff and I were eating strudel and drinking coffee in one of the few air-conditioned cafés along the single commercial street in Okahandja. Our waitress had a frown for a face and a white boss who stood behind the counter, gesturing rudely and shouting orders to the other waitresses in German.

"What's he saying?" I asked Pastor Cliff.

He shook his head. "I don't want to repeat it in English."

As we ate the sweet, greasy food, a legless man and a one-legged woman set up their beggars' camp across the road in front of a display of newspapers: *The Windhoek Advertiser, The Namibian, Allgemeine*

Zeitung. They used their makeshift stick crutches to lower themselves awkwardly to the ground, arranging their bodies on the sidewalk, arranging their cups in their hands, preparing to beg.

Watching these amputees extend their arms for change and charity, I felt ill. The skin on their forearms shook; their mouths twisted into sad faces of pleading. The line that separated me from them seemed so thin, and yet, at the moment, I could feel nothing but disgust for the way they looked, for the way their pants were filled with air, for the way they *were*—so deformed, so wrongly made, so incomplete. Normally, I never look at amputees. When I encounter legless beggars in the United States, I usually avert my eyes. I never look at my own body in a mirror, but here in Namibia I felt I was doing so. I watched these two the way others probably watched me when I wasn't careful to hide my disability. I could not avert my eyes.

Passersby gave money with a shy smile to the man, but they tossed the money at the woman's face. One man even spit on her. The woman lifted her head again and again, defiant. She looked down at the ground only to see what had been offered: money, empty wrappers, small puddles of spit.

Watching those amputees on that hot, muggy street while I sat, cool and comfortable behind the glass windows of the air-conditioned coffee shop, I felt implicated in their predicament. I was angry, and deeply, wretchedly afraid. I wasn't sure if these feelings came from a relief at my practical superiority to their situation, or if they came from the knowledge that my body, in this context, was really no different from theirs. I wanted those two people to disappear, and I felt horribly guilty for those feelings. The fact that I was on one side of the glass and those amputees were on the other was an accident of birth and passport alone.

My own accident at birth was a congenital defect that required my left leg to be amputated at age four. Although it had saddled me with a similarly disabled body, my American citizenship landed me on the inside of the café, sipping coffee from a clean porcelain cup while I watched these rag-clothed Namibian amputees beg for food outside, hands clenching broken Styrofoam cups. The idea that this all might simply be an issue of luck was troublesome to me.

I'd read up on Namibian history before arriving in Okahandja. The Nama and the Herero tribes fought throughout the 1800s, culminating in the Battle of Moordkoppie in 1850. More than seven hundred Herero men, women, and children were massacred by the Nama, who dismembered the Herero victims for the copper bangles worn on their arms and legs. As I watched the disabled woman across the street extend her shaking, emaciated arm, over and over again, I had visions of limbs carted off as war booty. I felt nauseated.

As Pastor Cliff and I walked back to camp, I thought about the privilege of a state-of-the-art prosthesis, and how having it literally set me free. The only things I do without my prosthesis are shower, have sex, and ski. The rest of the world sees only the transformed me, the able me that appears fully assembled and fully mobile. Although I resisted associations with those beggars, I also felt strangely aligned with them. This thought surprised and frightened me.

Inside I felt raw. Raw and mean. I rejected—yet also craved in some deep way—reminders of a body I wanted so badly to discard. For the rest of my trip, I never went back to that café, worried that I might see the disabled beggars again.

I do not know if this is true, but I was once told that almost every African language has a word for disabled people that means "stepped on by an animal"—an elephant, a lion, a wildebeest. Once, at a conference in Geneva, a Tanzanian woman approached me and said, "In my language 'disability' is like a curse word." She spoke to me in hushed tones as if she were invoking a demon. I felt immediately associated with what was broken, dirty, close to the ground, and closer to death. I was aware that there were millions of land mines in places like Angola, Zambia, Mozambique, Cambodia. Before I left for

Africa, I dragged around thick charts of statistics in clean white folders to present to people wearing white shirts and black suits. But I did
not identify with any of the people in the statistics.

Here in Namibia, I was white, rich, and well-dressed. I wore lip-
stick and had different clothes each day. Clean underwear. I was one
of the deformed and yet I was also privileged. Therefore I fit no category. I could not be defined, only named. Distrusted.

In America and Europe, I was used to being the one cast in the role
of victim. I was used to being the person who had the special ailment
to struggle against. I was used to my body acting as a mirror for others' worst fears of deformity, or what they viewed as an end to real or
normal or fulfilled life. I realized this had made me feel special; it had
given me a kind of collateral that I simply did not possess in Namibia.
I was not considered a victim here.

One Sunday I drove with a group of local women to church in
Pastor Cliff's battered, seat-belt-less van. Most of the women, many
of them younger than I, had several children back home and were
clearly delighted to have this time together. Their laughter and songs
were buoyant and infectious as we continued along the thin dusty
road into Windhoek, the absent windows letting in the warm morning air.

We visited a local city market where people sold their handmade
goods in front of the sleek display windows of The Gap. Clothes from
last year's catalogue graced the thin white mannequins. The women
placed smooth sculptures in my palm, closing my fingers around figures of elephants and lions, nodding their heads. Their fingers moved
over the object, over my own hands. I dangled an elephant from my
thumb. He was sleek and special—dark brown with a long, curved
tusk.

As we drove on to the church in a rural village, the perimeter of
Windhoek revealed to us its history of apartheid. Tarpaulin huts
were arranged alongside the road; gutters of sewage ran wickedly

through the unpaved dirt streets. A filthy girl with a straw twisted into her hair opened her rotted mouth and screamed at us. We heard dogs bark ferociously and then whine plaintively as if they'd just been kicked.

I later learned that colonizers had deliberately settled warring tribes next to each other. "To see if they would kill each other off," I was told. Tribes stacked upon tribes, in dominoes of hate. The townships of Goreangato, Wanaheda, Hakahana, and the southern areas of Katutura were high-crime areas characterized by boredom and unemployment. In all the guidebooks I read before my trip to Namibia, it was recommended that travelers avoid these areas. After Namibia's independence from South Africa, discrimination was officially illegal; yet in practice, it appeared that little had changed, at least geographically. In the center of town, near stores and cultural happenings, were the rich people—mostly white—living in stately houses surrounded by tall, impenetrable fences. These neighborhoods extended into formerly white-only suburbs with leafy streets and more high fences. Then there were the newer, middle-income suburbs, followed by the outlying all-black townships we drove through now.

The people in the settlements had a look of willful transience, of brave and reckless wandering, and yet they were confined to these spaces. The skin around their wide eyes sagged from malnutrition. Thin squatters picked through a fetid pool of garbage. We passed a tarpaulin hut. Two women sat on the ground in front of the entrance, one braiding the other's hair. In the rearview mirror, I watched one of the women throw an empty bottle at the van's wheels as we drove past.

I had seen extreme poverty before—kids standing ankle-deep in shit—viewed from a riverboat in Thailand. From that distance, I had been horrified and saddened, even shocked, but not deeply implicated in the people's lives or situation. Here, I was a white woman among African women in a van looking at a situation that was more than just a lack of services and goods. It was the product of a sinister institution. It was the kind of poverty built on nothing but the promise of eventual destruction.

I still do not know how to write or think about these moments. My privilege was like a sick fever I was grateful to have, a booty to grab and take with me on the plane *home*, a concept for which I was willing to barter anything in order to keep up the myth that this would never, ever happen to me.

I was so distracted by the surroundings and the feelings they aroused in me that I failed to notice that my skirt had fallen away from my legs, exposing the white skin of my right leg and the light brown hose that covered the prosthesis. Suddenly, I felt all eyes on my body. I kept looking out the window, where everything appeared unsafe, to avoid looking at the people who stared at me now. My face filled with heat as I felt their gaze and heard them murmuring.

Once we reached the church, the women piled out of the van and watched me climb out. Then they all seemed to prod one woman forward, as if they had chosen her as the communicator.

"Mine," she said, pointing at me. I was confused at first, but it suddenly dawned on me what she meant.

"No," I said, vigorously shaking my head. "Not a land mine."

She nodded as if I had not spoken. "Accident," she whispered. Her eyes glittered and I recognized the hunger in them—the hunger for the story, for the scandal.

"Birth," I replied.

She looked at me for a long time. "No," she said, moving her sandaled foot back and forth over the sand. She did not believe me. She turned her back to me and began talking to the women who stared at me.

"Birth," I said again to her back. I had meant to say it loud and strong, but the word came out soft and weak. I felt the women straining to hear something painful, something pornographic and scandalous. They wanted damage. I turned and set my face away from them. They could not have it.

Now or never, I thought. "Birth," I said under my breath for the rest of the day. "Birth." I felt deep anger at that woman for trying to call me out and make me ashamed. I suddenly wanted our van to fall in a hole somewhere, caught in the quagmires caused by the wet roads. I wanted to watch these women struggle, and then refuse to help them. I would stand back and judge them instead of letting them judge me.

In Geneva, the bus I took to work each morning made a stop in front of the United Nations. In the middle of the lawn in front of the sprawling white buildings was a giant three-legged chair, a sculpture that served as both a memorial for victims of land mines worldwide and a reminder that millions of mines still remained in the ground, waiting to kill and maim. When the bus approached that stop, I would look away as soon as I spotted the chair. I felt the need to straighten up, to somehow separate myself from those people who had lost legs to land mines. I'd seen the films—the sad, slow song playing as one-legged children, women, and men on crutches appeared on the screen. Such films were designed to arouse people's philanthropic tendencies by showing them a reflection of their fears. I knew the elimination of land mines was a worthy cause, and I wanted people to give money to stop the senseless carnage, but the films aroused strange emotions in me—anger, pity, shame. But when the bus pulled away from the chair, I always found myself wanting to turn back, wanting to look. However, I resisted; I didn't want anyone to mark my interest in this piece of artwork.

That day in Namibia, after our group returned from church, I sat down on my bunk and carefully painted my toenails and fingernails a rich, bright pink—a polish I'd bought at a ritzy store in Geneva, where the air was rich with the smell of chestnuts sold from barrels on the street. That nail polish nearly brought tears to my eyes. I felt the desire to be anywhere but here, but the here was my body. The promise of rain leaked through the walls. The sky was murky and muddy, too thick; it looked like I could stretch out my hand and grab great swaths of it, like taffy. My five bright pink toes twinkled, colorful, almost sinister, in the silver light.

By this point in my trip, I found that I had gotten used to the dark in Namibia, which seemed nothing short of a miracle. My life had never been my own in darkness; I had never been able to shake a childhood fear of what emerged from dark, unseen corners. Why, suddenly, was I not distraught when I reached out and could not see my hand several inches in front of my face? Maybe it was the swarm of warm breath in the cabin, the way it surrounded me like a heartbeat. At first it had been a disconcerting sound. I imagined all of us asleep in these log huts—asleep in the middle of Namibia, in the middle of Africa—where even our breath was exposed to one another. But the more I listened to it, the more it made me relax.

In the hot climate my leg gave off an odor of melting rubber and stale sweat, a smell of metal and oil, a smell that was not quite human. All around me were very human smells: laundered panties drying over the racks of bunks, stale unwashed underarms, hair oil melting into scalps. My smells were no less obvious and no more offensive than anybody else's. We were sweating, shitting, and showering together. We were locked in our own sleep and breath, together.

That night, like every other night, I waited until everyone else eased into sleep, and then I disassembled. Lying on my back, I carefully undid the Velcro of the socket, bit by bit, as quietly as possible so as not to wake anybody. I could not see what I was doing and had to go by feel alone. I worked in the dark, touching first the slightly rounded lip of the prosthesis, like rolled dough at the top of a piecrust, then the smooth thigh of silicone and plastic, hot to the touch. I worked my leg off under the covers and then sat back with relief. Fresh air! Out of the hot zone!

I ran my hands over my stump and worried over it. My stump resembled a baseball bat, chewed on where the scars are but rounded and smooth at the end, as if shaped by a potter's hand. It fit into the leg with a snap and a swoosh.

That night, enveloped in the thick, fog-like blackness of an African night, I learned that there is something spectacular, almost magical, about discovering your own shape in the dark, surrounded by the breath of others. Searching for the shape of your body with your hands is like using a key to hunt for a lock in deep, deep darkness. With my hands I found my disabled body in a mysterious, quiet space. For the first time in my life, I secretly—guiltily—rejoiced, although I had been claiming for years that I loved my body. The fear of darkness had always been linked to the fear of my own body. But I now discovered that my body was something strange, yet wondrous, to behold. That night was the beginning of a kind of re-creation, a rebirth. Words that shaped first in my mouth, then eased into my body, and then finally moved into the world, began in that darkness: *My Body. Mine.*

No Other Joy

DBDSN (STEENABLOG.BLOGSPOT.COM)

If you know no other this year, know this one: the day off for an appointment. The lovely dark-haired doctor, tall and in Wisconsin-sensible shoes, admits to tanning the night before. She admires your red Chucks for what they are: canvas impracticality. At noon, light all the candles in the apartment and play Aretha on the record player the way your mother would have, then light yourself cigarette after daytime cigarette. When the snow begins to fall—movie-flakes—pour a tumbler of coffee vodka. Raise a toast to small victories. Later you take yourself out to lunch at the type of place where the staff wear suspenders, and if anyone were to see you and your love walking through the neon drifts, your fingers in his pockets, they would think you happy: your shoes, bright cardinals underfoot.

First Year

LAURA BRAMON GOOD

"Finding blood on our basement apartment walls was like receiving solemn instruction to keep searching for meaning in the heartbreaking stories—our own and others—that haunted my husband, Ben, and me during our first year of marriage," says Laura Bramon Good. "There had to be a reason, beyond the gut punch of fear and sorrow . . . Ben and I now live in an urban family commune with two other married couples and their children. When 'First Year' was published in Image, *I put the journal on the coffee table and invited my roommates to read it. One of their questions was: why would I publish something so personal and private? In part, it's because once I had mapped the pain and sense of that year, the experiences revealed their beauty and their meaning—both of which were worth sharing, either for the chance to behold or the chance to learn."*

We don't notice the bloodstains when we first walk through the apartment. We notice the crumbling holes in the walls—small puncture wounds along the alcove where a bed might fit, a crusty gash where the toilet paper holder has been ripped out of the wall—but we don't ask. We are sweating in the white-walled, windowless basement apartment: my husband, Ben, and I, along with our red-faced retiree landlord-to-be and his quiet wife. Around us stands the debris of a very feminine life: metal buckets of fake lavender, a tall shelf full of books on women's rights and poetry. Two matching papasan chairs stare at a TV; cute shoes lie matched in an open closet.

"We'll fix those," the landlord says, gesturing to the holes, looking to my husband. "Of course, we'll fix those."

The next week, the apartment is empty and the holes in the walls are matte spots so cleanly leveled that I do not see them unless, as I pass, I see the light change on the face of the paint. My husband and I walk through the bare rooms and try to imagine where our boxes and borrowed furniture will go. In the bathroom, we stand surveying the cramped appointments. Ben reaches out and takes hold of the cheap, stretched roller shade hanging askew from the window. His thumb rubs a dark, almost brown streak on the shade; his eyes pause for a moment before tracking to a set of dark spots on the ceiling.

"It's blood," he says.

"Really?" I stare at the shade in his hand and look up at the ceiling, trying to imagine what kind of an accident would fling blood to both surfaces.

"I think it is," he says.

Later, putting groceries away, my hand hits a patch of brownish spots on the freezer door, spackled around and behind the door handle. With my fingernail, I chip at the stain, then, remembering the spots in the bathroom, I rub hard, trying to forget what they might be.

THE WOMAN WHO lived here last was a waitress. Her boyfriend was a rapper. She was Russian; he was black. The apartment was in her name, but he lived here most of the time, too, the girls who rent the upstairs tell us. Many nights the two of them stood together in the wide main basement room, hooting and keening, doing vocal exercises to prepare for his performances. I almost laugh when the girls tell me this; I imagine a slender white woman and a shirtless, lean man standing crouched before each other like animals, intense and absurd and very serious. She is in a tank top; her pale stomach shows. He can't be too big; his fists, like the holes in the wall, are small. But I can't divine a face for either; the expressions and features are smudged and particulate, taking pieces from the faces of boys I knew in junior high, teenage girls I have seen in the mall chattering in slippery Russian.

I ask the girls upstairs if they ever heard anything: screaming, crying, arguing. Beyond a final fight, they say, and the barking vocalises, they did not hear or see much of either the woman, who would not look them in the eye as she walked down the driveway to her door, or the man, who came and went in the middle of the night in a battered black car.

THE CEILING OF the basement apartment is thick enough to give us muted sounds from upstairs of feet treading, the floor creaking, water shushing on and off in the kitchen sink. Walking the small, walled horseshoe of basement rooms while carrying laundry to the bed or shoes to the closet, I never hear voices. Once in a while I hear a sneeze or a cough. I wonder what they hear of us.

In our last apartment, a coast away, the long bedroom window opened to a ruined garden that nobody, save a crying dog, ever visited. The ground rose in a bowl and the sounds of life in the other apartments rolled and floated in it: one person tinkering in a room, one door easing open and shut, one man who talked to himself in a high, mocking voice and then sang, full-throated, for hours. When Ben and I fought in the evenings, we could hear a faint echo of our voices reverberate in that open space. Later, as we lay in bed exhausted with anger or perhaps repentance, the breeze from that window would bring the reply of a small child's cries. She was somewhere in our building, calling out not in pain or anger, but in a kind of elated defiance. Her voice seemed close to a window, as if she were standing on a bed, holding onto the chipping tile window ledge as she stared out into the dark and screamed.

WE FIND BLOOD on other things in the apartment: a doorjamb, the metal hatch that hides the electrical panel, a low space on a bedroom wall. Every surface is white; the blood is inky brown, spattered and feathery or congealed in long teardrops as it fell. Often, Ben and I find the blood together as we are completing a task. We see it, stare at it, and say nothing. His thumb will rush to pick or press at the blood, wiping it without a word. One morning, I stumble to the dim bathroom and I can see, even in the dark, that he has washed the blood off the shade and ceiling. A muddy bruise still stains the hatched plastic fabric of the curtain.

We fight on Sunday afternoons, perhaps because his school studies and my long days of work leave us little time to bicker on the weekday evenings. We sit across from each other in the main basement room: one on the couch, one in an old orange chair. He is stony; I shriek. He finally shouts and I cry, the sound chiming flatly against the low ceiling. I think briefly but blankly of the house above us and what it can hear.

In the aftermath, we get up and pass each other without a word. There is nothing: no footsteps, voices, heartbeats of washers or dryers or sucking pipes. The quiet of the house seems as conspicuous as the hush of a crowd—as if, even though we are alone, we are watched.

THERE ARE IN fact three windows in the "windowless" apartment, three small, shaded portholes we could bust, if lucky, and shimmy through to escape fire or smoke. Waking up on a Monday after a fight, staring into the flat darkness, I often wish for the light of our old apartment's windows: not only the long garden window, but also the full bank of windows that filled the front of the apartment with sun and a view of a street and the fog and cranes of a canal.

I looked out these wide front windows one evening and saw the little girl who screamed at night. She ran past our apartment, chased by her mother. Her father's hoarse voice shouted out at her from the open door of the apartment next to ours, a huge end unit where three college boys lived. He visited them often. Craning my head from where I stood cooking dinner in our corridor kitchen, I watched the little girl run back and forth as she and her mother yelled at each other. The little girl had dark hair, her tiny ponytail still soft with new curls that shook as she ran.

Soon, the men came out to smoke and crowded against our window, blocking the late evening light. Inside our apartment, I stepped closer to them, catching glimpses of the little girl standing amidst their legs. Her mother was there, too, reaching a hand down to her daughter, the tops of her dangling breasts fat and chapped, looking like fruit gone veiny and bad at the skin but still thick and ripe at the heart. Above the mother's breasts were small eyes; somewhere in between was her mouth, open, laughing, almost panting. The father's mouth was like this, too, but cracking out of a black-stubbled face that I would never see clean-shaven. Later, I would glimpse the tattoo portraits on their calves: his of her, hers of him, their plain features caricatured in doe-eyed, dreamy busts.

THE MOTHER WAS young, no more than twenty-two, I guessed, and likely lying when she told me she was married. I had known girls like her; in adolescence, I had been shy and shadowed by them, jealously loved by them, and, in turn, obsessed and bored and frightened by their sadness and their stories. Later that week while Ben and I fought, I imagined the mother in their east-end apartment, lying on a messy bed, humoring the little girl's play and listening to our high-pitched cries, sounds that might at first have been mistaken for the birds that dipped down into the garden at dusk. The next morning I heard a knock on the front window, and before I opened the door, I could smell her standing there: a moldering scent of must and smoke and cheap food, like a familiar perfume whose presence piques the body with a sharp, almost sexual fear.

She was standing on the doormat in her socks, eyes dizzy and skin ruddy with sleep. It was ten o'clock. Her red hair was matted at the temples and she wore her husband's loose, studded leather jacket over a T-shirt and plaid flannel pants. She remembered my name. It took me a minute to remember hers.

"Can I use your cell?" Jessie asked, holding out her hand.

"Sure." I gave it to her.

"Thanks," she waved, padding back down to her apartment, where the door was still open. I could hear the TV's music and the little girl's brief, demanding yell.

In a couple of minutes Jessie was back, the silver phone warm with the heat of her hand. I felt it cool by grades in my own as she stood in the doorway, talking idly, the unsure focus of her eyes hovering at my ears, the crown of my head, my neck. She was talking about her mother, her sister, someone she had called to ask for money, but the conversation seemed little more than a scheme to stare at me. Once, her gaze caught mine, probing and passing so quickly that I felt a pang of shame, as if she knew something and were testing to see if I could tell. I thought of last night's fight, only hours past. I imagined that she had truly heard us.

WALKING PAST JESSIE'S apartment on the days I worked, I peered through the blinds on their long windows and saw the same

corridor kitchen, living room, and bedroom hallway of our home.
The warm air rimming their apartment smelled like her and I walked
through it quickly, barely breathing as I surveyed the toy-littered
floor and the opalescent eye of a huge TV. Sometimes I saw food on
the kitchen counter—a white bowl, an orange-hued, slumping bag
of bread—but usually it was empty. The morning Jessie came to our
apartment and asked for food, I tried to make kind small talk as she
stood awkwardly in our kitchen, waiting for me to fill a plastic sack
with apples, cheese, and the green and white packs of butchered game
we had brought back from home. It was the last of the meat. I was
barely making minimum wage; Ben worked day labor on a construc-
tion crew. It was hard for me to slip it into the sack.

She took the bag and left quickly. The next day, she brought it all
back.

"Joe's dad sent us money," she said. "I told you I'd pay you back."
She handed me the bags and stood in the doorway, talking hungrily as
she had the first time she knocked. I could smell her smoky scent rising
faintly from the food in the bag. Her eyes roamed me and the rest of
the room; I knew that she wanted to come in. I didn't want to let her.

I was sitting at my living room desk later that week staring out
the wide front window, shades half-closed, when I heard a door
bang open and small feet slap down the walkway. Suddenly, the little
girl stood at the top of the west-end stairs, only a few feet from me.
Through the thin pane, I could hear her breathe.

"Izzie!" Jessie yelled. "Izzie."

A grating rumble grew louder as Jessie walked past pulling a plastic
laundry bin, dingy clothes and sheets bulging from the flower-shaped
cutouts. She was wearing Joe's jacket, and the metal studs clanged
against the rail as she jarred the bin down the stairs, grabbed Izzie's
hand, and shook her.

I was still sitting at my desk a couple of hours later as Jessie began
to bring clean, dry laundry back up to their apartment. Her arms were

full when Joe bounded up the stairs behind her, passed her without a word, then whirled around and backed her against the rail. I couldn't hear what he said, but I caught plainly her apologetic mewing and his final, harsh shout. She did not look up when he turned away and ran down the walkway to their door.

THE NEXT TIME I saw Jessie, she was hunched at the bus stop late on Friday afternoon. Her red hair hung frizzy in the fog and her leather jacket was pulled up around her shoulders. I was lugging grocery bags filled with wine, bread, and a few other things we needed for a dinner party. When I said hello, she glanced up and looked away as if she had not seen me.

"Hey, Izzie's at your house," she said, staring out at the street. "Joe's in jail. I just have to go down with some papers." She stepped out into the street to look for the bus. "I know you've got friends coming over, so."

She did not turn around as I said goodbye.

Up at our apartment, the windows were bright and the glass was glazed with heat from the kitchen. When I knocked, Izzie opened the door. Flecks of dried gravy colored her lips and chin; I touched her head, briefly grasping the soft curls, and brought the grocery bags into the kitchen. Ben leaned close to kiss me and said: "Joe's in jail."

"I know. I saw Jessie at the bus," I said.

"They had a fight."

His words hung in the air. We had fought hard, stupidly, a couple of nights before. I had thrown something; he had grabbed my wrists to try to stop me, at once furious and protective. We had struggled. We had never done this before.

"Izzie's okay?"

"She looks fine. Jessie's neck's all bruised."

I put the wine on the counter and slipped a heavy, round loaf of bread from its brown bag. I tried to think if I had seen Jessie's neck; it had been hidden in the jacket's flipped-up collar.

"What happened?"

"He got drunk or high with the guys next door and then—I don't know. I think he came back and tried to hurt her and she stabbed him and called the police. It was late last night," he said. It sounded almost comical, false as he reeled it off.

"Did you hear anything?" I said.

"No."

The carpet banking the kitchen was littered with pieces of blue notepaper, each branded with Izzie's sharp, circular scrawl. I picked up the papers, feeling the ridged abrasions on the back of each note. Some of them she had punctured over and over again with the pen. I looked up and saw her sitting under the folding table Ben had set up for dinner, singing to herself as she marched a marble up the table leg. I watched her, her face's usual hard expression softened a bit in the privacy of play.

The dinner was an engagement party for a friend. I set the table around Izzie, who seemed content to stay beneath it as I spread out a tablecloth and set six places of our white and silver wedding china. When my friends began to arrive, Ben beckoned her out from underneath the table. She stared at the guests and stood beside him in the kitchen while he finished preparing the meal.

Jessie knocked on the window just as we sat down for dinner. When I opened the door, her face was damp and pale yellow under the fluorescent walkway light. She was not wearing her leather jacket.

"Would you like to come in?" I asked her. I meant it.

"No," she said, her gaze hovering and indirect. "I left all my papers on the bus in my coat. So we're kind of screwed." She laughed hoarsely. "I need to find a phone."

I grabbed our cell phone off the desk and gave it to her, and she and Izzie left.

During the party, the apartment windows remained cloudy with heat. I saw Jessie's vague form run back and forth beyond the glass, Izzie's feet slapping and their voices yelling as we drank and laughed, raising our glasses in toasts to our friend and to love, fidelity, and children to come.

THE DAYS WANED quickly that weekend. By five o'clock each evening the bushes and trees of the garden grew shadowed and sedentary, like animals bedding down for the night. Lights from the ground-floor windows lit the saplings in the garden's trench, so I could tell when Jessie and Izzie were home and when they were gone. I could see their light late into the night and hear their yelling voices, which I mistook once for echoes of our own.

We didn't see them on Sunday. On Monday, they knocked at our front window. I could hear them breathing and bickering as I peered through the slit blinds. They stood pale and sleepy, still dressed in their pajamas in the early afternoon. Once inside, Jessie sat at the table, not eating, not drinking. I sat across from her, watching the blue and brown bruises on her neck ripple as she swallowed and stared. Izzie played at our feet, flaying the same blue notepad, littering the room with its ragged squares.

"My grandfather died," Jessie finally said, "with my mouth on his."

Why are you telling me this? I wanted to ask. But I said nothing as she recounted how her father and uncle had refused to obey the dispatcher's orders, so she, barely twelve, had clamped the phone to one ear, pumped her grandfather's chest with her fist, and breathed into his cocked mouth. "When I did it, his breath came out of him and I tasted everything he had eaten," she said. "Chicken. We had had it for dinner."

She sat in the chair staring, talking about her mother, her sister, and finally about Joe, how she and he and Izzie had come to the city with some cash left over from her grandfather's money. "Then he couldn't get a job," she said, "and he made me dance." She cried hard for a moment.

"Did he hurt you before?" I asked.

"No," she said. "Yes. I hurt him." She was touching the bruises, fingering them as if they were the beads of a necklace. "I love him," she said.

WHILE JESSIE TALKED, I watched the window behind her, the sky darkening early as a spate of gray clouds rolled in and dropped cold, spitting rain, stopping the traffic and filling the road below us with crawling red taillights. I thought about the fight Ben and I had had a couple of nights before Joe attacked Jessie. I tried to remember what I had needed from Ben, what he had done to hurt me, but I had forgotten. What I remembered was the heady swell of anger and the thrill of lunging to hurl anything across the room. I remembered Ben's face blanking in fear, his hands catching my wrists; I wrestled free, screaming and feeling in my stomach the sick terror of having urged each other to this.

I remembered too the first real fight of our marriage, on a snowy morning in a partitioned old house where we first lived. Its other inhabitants were silent as we quarreled and then yelled in the dark. I hit him for the first time: a dull, childish bat against his chest, and I was startled by how physically weak I was against him and by the intense warmth of his body. I came home from work early that day and lay in a scalding bath. I thought of our fight and of my parents' fights, the addicting griefs and reunions of their bitter quarrels. Even then, years from home, the memory made me want to vomit. When Ben came home from work, we reconciled. But we fought again before the sun went down, and as I mocked him I could feel my anger rising even faster than it had before, breathless and ruthless and wishing he would stop me.

BEN GOT HOME late. When he came in, Jessie was still sitting at the table and Izzie was asleep on the futon. We were quiet as he stamped the loose mud off his pants and peeled off his work boots.

"You're here for dinner?" he asked her.

"Sure," she said.

Jessie roused Izzie and took my phone, and they went home to make a call before dinner. I put water on for pasta and stood staring at the stovetop, numb with everything Jessie had told me and with what had played through my mind as she talked. I listened to Ben in the shower, the sound of the water echoing and distant, and I wandered to the bathroom door. It was warm with the heat of the small room; steam seeped over me as I opened it. Ben had just shut off the water and was standing naked, wrapping the towel around his waist. I stepped through the haze and set my face on his damp chest and started to cry. He wrapped his arms around me. He sighed deeply and I could feel his chest shudder, too.

I THINK OF this moment while I am standing at the bathroom mirror in the basement apartment. Its silver glass is hazy with spittle and grimy dust, and just fogged at the edges with the last of the steam from my shower. My hair is wet; my body is damp and cold. Ben is gone after a fight. Is it possible, I ask myself, staring at the pale skin, the fine lines ridging my forehead, to love? I remember the feeling of his wet chest hair against my face and the slow fumbling that led us to the bed, and how we could hear Jessie and Izzie's shouting, crying voices as we made love.

I reach down under the cabinet to pull up the glass cleaner and paper towels that the Russian girl left behind. The paper towels are as thick and soft as real cloth, and the cleaner is expensive and sweet-smelling, a brand I would never pay to buy but that I have used gladly, with a satisfaction that turns grim when I remember why she left. We have been receiving her mail: stacks and stacks of home decorating magazines that show china-laden tables, wide armchairs, meals set in perfect gardens. I have been poring over the magazines, thinking of them in her hands, wondering what she would have lingered over.

I wander through the cluttered bedroom and living room to the kitchen and take a stiff scrubbing pad from the kitchen sink. I will use it to clean the shower, I think. Then I will bleach it and put it back. Walking back through the rooms slowly, my hands reach out to touch the walls, and I remember each place where we have cleaned up her blood. For a moment, I feel that I am trespassing in her small space. It belongs to us now, I think reasonably. She is somewhere else. Her father came to get her, our landlord said, and took her home.

I remember Jessie and Joe's front door standing open a crack, breathing with the wind on the walkway after Joe had come home from jail and they had been evicted. The door was open for over a week before Ben decided to go into their apartment. I followed him, letting him step first into the rooms and flash on each overhead light. In the living room, the huge TV stood glassy and blank before strewn clothes and toys. The kitchen was bare; the bathroom was dirty. In the bedroom, a giant battleship model lay large and gray on the unmade bed.

"I had this one when I was a kid," Ben said. He picked up the ship, inspecting it. I stood by the bedroom door, watching him, surveying the room and glancing out into the garden through the long bedroom window.

In the dresser at my side, a half-crumpled piece of paper stuck out of the top drawer. I pulled it free and unfolded it. It was a computer-printed snapshot of a young woman, her hair curled and teased, her smile wide in a round, sweet face. A chunky, fake-diamond necklace was clasped at her thin neck. It was Jessie.

"Look," I said.

I kept it in my hand while Ben led me through each room again, shutting off all the lights.

Just outside their door, he turned to me. On the threshold of the apartment, half in the dark and half in the streetlight, I saw his face's lines more deeply and clearly, his features both unmasked and distorted. He was close to me; he touched my face. I could smell the house's dank scent milking out into the night, mingling with the cool, humid air of the city and the faint musk of Ben's body. I imagined how my own face must have looked to him, similarly strange and clear, and I closed my eyes while he ran his hand over my cheeks and temples as if they were a map. When I opened my eyes, he was still watching me. I reached up and kissed him as he pulled the door firmly shut.

Letter from a Japanese Crematorium

MARIE MUTSUKI MOCKETT

Part of the appeal of creative nonfiction is that, unlike journalism, it allows the writer to become a part of the story, a freedom Marie Mutsuki Mockett initially resisted when writing this story about her grandmother's funeral. "When I turned in an early draft of this essay, my agent asked for a rewrite," Mockett recalls. "She asked, 'Where are all those fun details?' She reminded me of how I had told her the story . . . in a rush after returning from Japan. In the first draft of my essay, I'd explained what happened in a crematorium and at a funeral, but left out my grandmother's secrets, the admonition from my mother's friends and my grandfather's emotional speech. I resisted making any edits at first; I didn't want to write down my personal observations. But as I ruminated, the essay took on a kind of shape in my mind, rounded out by the details I'd suppressed. . . . In my writing process I find that I still go through these two stages: an inert factual phase, followed by a revealing one." The story appeared in AGNI.

My cousin Takahagi, a Buddhist priest, does not want me to go to the crematorium. It is not a place for visitors. When I press him, he explains: the crematorium is a gateway to the next world and is potentially dangerous. In Japan, cremation is avoided on certain days of the week, known as *tomobiki*, or "friend-pulling" days. If you cremate a body on tomobiki, the soul that is finally and forcibly removed from the flesh might snatch along a family member or friend for company.

Despite the impression you might have from certain Hollywood films, most Buddhist priests do not contentedly live on remote mountaintops waiting to dispense spiritual advice to depressed sons of millionaires who secretly long to be superheroes. The priests I know are busy with paperwork, scheduling, and appointments. Their job is to oversee everything related to death and rebirth, which, in Japan, is an elaborate, continuous, and expensive process.

I know something about temples and priests because my Japanese family owns a Buddhist temple, which my great-grandfather took over in the late nineteenth century. Our temple is part of the Sōtō sect, which Americans know of as Zen. My grandfather, once slated to inherit the complex, rebelled, leaving the temple in the hands of his sister, whose son has run it successfully for the past thirty years. Now *his* twenty-five-year-old son, Takahagi (technically my second cousin, but to simplify things, I'll refer to him as my cousin), is poised to continue the family tradition.

Takahagi has come to pick me up from Iwaki train station, which is located north of Tokyo and not far from Sendai city. He cuts an elegant figure on the other side of the exit gate with his black fedora, black narrow-ankle jeans, and gossamer black T-shirt bearing a print of a skull. He is also sporting a pair of pointy-toed shoes that he found on a day trip to Harajuku; he will shop for street clothes only in Tokyo. His most prized possession is an American Chevrolet, which, he tells me proudly, was once a hearse. He purchased it from a guy who claims to have bought it from the army base in Okinawa, then transported it to the main island of Honshu. Indeed, when I look back at the cabin, it does have fat, cavernous proportions capable of holding an American coffin.

Lately Takahagi has been thinking of selling the hearse because it guzzles too much gas, and because every time he wants to get out of a parking lot he has to climb over to the passenger side to retrieve a ticket from the automated ticket dispenser. The other day the police stopped to talk to him when the hearse stalled on the expressway. He explained to them that he was a priest, but they didn't believe him at first because so many kids these days shave their heads as a fashion statement.

I can't help but wonder if Takahagi's early and constant exposure to death hasn't colored his sensibilities in some way. His older brother has become that Japanese social pariah, the *otaku*, who hides away in his room playing video games and conversing with characters in comic books. As the oldest son, my otaku cousin was supposed to take over the temple, but his extreme antisocial behavior makes this transition unlikely. As Takahagi navigates the country road around the contours of emerald rice paddies, he cheerfully waves to the parishioners and they wave back. No sullen Goth is he, but a fashionable young man whose stylish eccentricities are to be indulged for the moment.

When we reach the temple, where his parents live and the rest of the family is waiting, Takahagi slips into a side room and changes into his official "casual priest clothing," which looks like a pair of pajamas with elastic around the wrists and ankles. Outfits like these are ordered from a Buddhist catalogue that sells, among other things, incense, new sutras, and gongs.

I've been visiting the temple over many years, but this trip is significant because I have come for my grandmother's funeral. My ninety-three-year-old grandfather and other family members have already arrived from various parts of Japan and are now waiting for me. Most of them attended the earlier funerary rites before my arrival, including the cremation that has so piqued my curiosity.

During dinner, my family—my grandfather, uncles, mother, and cousins—eat a spread of sashimi and vegetables, and the discussion continually returns to the impending funeral, which carries the conversational weight of an anchor. I imagine that a stranger peering through a window might find us all unremarkable, but the truth is that beneath the surface pleasantry lies an unvoiced secret. My grandmother, born to an aristocratic family that slowly lost its fortune during Japan's wrenching transformation to modernity, married my grandfather less for love than for money and stability.

It was a union that produced three children but, as my grandmother liked to whisper to me late at night as we lay in our futons, little happiness. My grandfather, a brilliant but strict man, was given to violent outbursts and seemingly capricious mood swings. Like many mercurial personalities, he is highly charismatic, and he channeled his talents into the teaching of English. His students used to ask me if I was afraid of him. I always lied and boasted that I was not. Now that I have reached my Amazonian height of five-foot-five, I am not as afraid of my grandfather as I once was.

Before my grandmother died, she asked her children to return her remains to her aristocratic, natal plot. Her parents and servants are buried there, and she wanted to be with them. Then as now, my mother finds this request egotistical and is disgusted that her brothers indulged it. Japanese tradition dictates that a family be buried together so that it can be honored during important holidays. It's an arrangement few people question, just as they would not think of wearing shoes on a tatami floor. Moreover, my mother hates deceiving her father, who knows nothing of the secret pact. Before the funeral, I'm of the opinion that if an elaborate subterfuge is required to send my grandmother back home, then so be it.

During dinner my mother redirects her frustration to the post-funeral-luncheon seating chart because it places her sister-in-law in a comparatively senior position. At this, my uncle moans that beer is in order, and my clean-living grandfather roars that if we do not learn to behave correctly in this world, he will come back as a ghost to torture us all.

The men shift uncomfortably on their *zabuton* pillows. My otaku cousin wanders down to gobble his dinner in silence before parking himself in front of the television to debate with then–Prime Minister Koizumi, who is on the evening news. Takahagi's mother chafes at having so many people in her house at once, and every now and then a dish she is washing rattles against its neighbor.

The meal ends with no satisfying conclusion. One by one the men drift off to smoke, or, in my uncle's case, to sneak a case of beer out of the refrigerator in the temple's adjoining meeting hall. Eventually, I'm alone with Takahagi. In this precious hour of privacy, we talk about his secret girlfriend and my secret boyfriend. Then I ask him about the crematorium.

Here is what I learn:

Cremation was once reserved for nobles but is now mandatory in most of Japan. It is also only one part of the expensive funeral process. In 2004 the average funeral in Japan cost 1.65 million yen, or $14,000, almost four times the average funeral in the United States. A significant portion of this money goes to the priest, which accounts for the Mercedes-Benz that Takahagi's father drove for half a year until complaints from his parishioners made him give it up for a Toyota. The funeral industry in Japan is evolving as demographics and ties to tradition change, so prices are slowly falling. But there are still plenty of families in the rural, thus more traditional parts of Japan (our family temple is located in such a place) who wouldn't be caught dead with anything less than the full after-life treatment.

Cremation generally takes about an hour, with an extra thirty minutes or so added on to give the remains time to cool. The ovens reach a peak heat of 500 to 600 degrees Celsius, which is substantially cooler than in the Western process. In Japan, it is important to preserve some bone. There will be no sterile handing-off of a small urn, no dispensing of powdery ash into the ocean.

While the flesh dissolves, unseen attendants keep watch. Some monitor the security of the building by means of cleverly hidden cameras, in case a grieving family member returns to the oven unaccompanied to try to rescue the body. After about an hour, an attendant will go to a hidden chamber behind the ovens and look through a tiny fireproof window to see just how much is left of the cremated corpse, making adjustments as necessary.

"There's a window?" I ask.

"There has to be," Takahagi nods. "What if there is a problem and the body is only half-cremated when the family goes to pull out the bones?"

"The family retrieves the body?"

"Of course. You can't let strangers handle something so personal."

Then I ask him again if he will take me to visit the local crematorium, and offer my standard armchair anthropologist's shtick about how I admire Japan's ability to combine technological prowess with a fastidious intolerance of germs and waste. Consider, for example, the toilet down the hall, which has all the features you hear about on blogs and in the news: a bidet function, a selection of noises—waterfall, toilet flush—to mask the sound of urination should one be embarrassed by such things, a perpetually heated seat. ("You mean American toilets aren't like that?" My cousin is incredulous.) More seriously, I remind him that, until recently, leather workers, butchers, and undertakers were relegated to an outcast status in Japan; their work with death and meat was considered a pollutant. I wonder how, if at all, the modern crematorium is more viable in such a purity-obsessed but democratic society.

A conversation I had a few days before arriving at the temple comes to mind. I was at Chita Peninsula, which is south of the city of Nagoya, with my mother, who was born there. Like the century-old houses that dot the landscape, she was able to escape the bombings that decimated so many of Japan's cities during the war. We visited an *onsen*, or hot-spring spa, with one of my mother's childhood friends. They are two of a kind, a pair of sylphlike creatures chattering about high-school days and the healing properties of vinegar, while I, with my pink skin and muscular frame, am quite obviously not fully Japanese.

When my mother left the onsen to try the sauna, my mother's friend turned to me and murmured, "There are many things you can't understand about Japan. You aren't going to be able to help your mother right now. You must let people like me take care of her. You can take care of her in America."

I felt sideswiped. It isn't completely true, what they tell you about Japanese people being habitually vague. Once you speak the language, a whole world of strong emotion and color opens up to you.

"She was my grandmother, too," I finally said.

"Look. Don't be hard on yourself. We don't expect you to understand us." She turned her back to me and paddled out of the water to join my mother.

This is something one hears in Japan from time to time: that those of us who aren't one hundred percent Japanese can't appreciate the full range of Japanese cuisine and taste it the way they do, that we aren't able to relate to other Japanese people during *Obon* or a *matsuri*. It's a judgment I resist. I've always bridged the two worlds my mother occupies. It's a responsibility I take seriously, perhaps even more seriously than my father does. After all, I'm the one who speaks both languages, who knows how to take off my shoes at the entrance to a house without falling over, how to sense the amount of personal space around me on a crowded train, how to be moved by a *hototo-gisu* singing in the twilight. If there is something new to grasp about Japan, I have the reflexive impulse to do so.

And the fact is, because I speak Japanese yet remain something of an outsider, I generally end up hearing the things that are considered taboo. A family friend confided that he might be bisexual; then he broke down and confessed he was actually gay (and could he stay with me in New York for three months to experience liberation?). My mother's cousin, who I'd always been told was adopted, revealed to me in the five minutes it took to walk to the house from the park-ing lot where we had bidden goodbye to guests that he was actually the illegitimate son of my grandfather's brother, and therefore my blood relative. When I was twelve, my grandmother showed me an old photo of a handsome young man and told me that he was her "true love." It was not a photo of my grandfather. With geographical, not to mention cultural, distance, secrets mistakenly appear to lose their power.

Despite all this, Takahagi remains unconvinced. "I am sorry. I just wouldn't feel comfortable taking you for a visit to the crematorium," says my cousin, driver of the American hearse.

IN THE MORNING, I find my way to the local crematorium on my own just fine. It is a stark, one-story building concealed inside a coil of trees and bamboo, in a remote part of town accessible only by automobile. The brooding copper brow of a roof hangs low over a dark, marble entrance.

Automated doors slide open, and an attendant, wearing what looks like a conductor's uniform complete with cap and gloves, glides out of the entryway. I give him my spiel. I'm here from America, obviously, and want to know more about the inner workings of a crematorium, as I missed my grandmother's cremation. He nods, as if this is a perfectly reasonable request, then advises me to wait. A mourning party is scheduled to arrive in five minutes and he must prepare.

I watch him wheel a specially designed handcart out to the sloped sidewalk. The cart is a marvel of engineering with hydraulic lifts and an automated conveyor belt. When the hearse arrives, with its gold-and-black headdress elaborately carved like a temple roof, the attendant bows, and easily extracts the coffin from the back.

It is quiet inside the marble hallway. Two rows of indoor street lamps shine a luminous pathway on the floor. A priest and the party of mourners follow as the attendant gravely steers the coffin through this solemn space. The women are wearing black kimonos made of silk so heavy it seems to ooze like ink in the atmospheric light. I watch as high doors open at the far end of the hall and swallow the mourning party. The quiet returns once they are gone, save the faint sounds of a chanting priest and a ringing bell.

I retire to a small cafeteria, which is selling noodles and tea and offers a view of a rock garden. It is a pleasant enough space, resembling a hotel or, perhaps more accurately, an airport lobby, down to the video screens displaying the names of those whose remains are ready for pickup. In the distance I can hear the hum of other guests who have rented out a private waiting room with tatami mats and zabuton pillows. They are cloistered together, perhaps eating a specially designed funeral bento, so designated because it contains nary a speck of meat—only fish, rice, and vegetables. In another wing, someone is cremating a pet dog.

The glove-and-cap-clad attendant comes to get me, checking his watch. The crematorium has been carefully designed to function as a series of systems, he says brightly. There are multiple pathways that enable him to direct all parties through the same ritualized experience while avoiding undesirable traffic jams. He has fifteen minutes to give me a tour.

He leads me from the main hall into the second room—a sort of intermediary chamber—where a shrine is laden with numerous bouquets of yellow and white chrysanthemums and a portrait of the man who has just been sent to the crematorium. He is perhaps in his sixties, smiling and healthy—a father, husband, and grandfather to all those who brushed past me in the main hall. He loved cigarettes, baseball, and golf books, all of which have been placed on the altar. It occurs to me that I have crashed a funeral and I start to feel guilty that my curiosity has led me to invade what is surely the most intimate and private of spaces.

In a third chamber, the steel jaws of twelve small ovens are clamped shut. Because the crematorium regularly processes more than one body at a time, heat-resistant digital screens above each oven display the name of the temporary occupant so that there will be no confusion. The casket is slid inside under the somber gaze of the mourners, and the head of the family is charged with locking the door and pocketing the key—the only one, he is told, that can open this particular oven. Before the mourners leave the stark room for the waiting area, they hear the breath of gas and the snarl of fire as the casket, flowers, and body are consumed.

There is only one thing that modern engineering cannot dispense with, and that is the smell. After visiting the crematorium, I won't eat meat for several weeks.

The attendant takes me to a clean, stark space that looks more like an empty hospital room than the grand marble chambers I've just seen. This is the bone-picking room. Two weeks ago, while I was in America, my grandfather was led away solo from the waiting room to open up the oven with his special key. When my mother joined him a few minutes later, she said she found him standing in this room, warming his hands over my grandmother's remains, which lay stretched out on a steel table. This, the attendant tells me, is not so unusual; there are some who even eat from the bones of the deceased, or request a cup of water to make a kind of tea.

My uncle had joined my grandfather to begin the intimate process of picking out bones, each using a pair of unusually long chopsticks. They started with the feet first so my grandmother would not be upside down in her rectangular urn, which is about as large as an ice-cream tub. This is the only time that two people will hold anything together using chopsticks, hence the reason the Japanese flinch if two people inadvertently reach down to pick up the same morsel of food from a plate. An attendant in the background identified each bone. "Here is the second joint of the big toe." "Here is a fragment of a femur." At the top were pieces of my grandmother's skull, jaw, and the all-important hyoid bone from the Adam's apple, which will rest in a separate box. So many of my grandmother's bones survived the cremation that we were given a third urn.

"She must have been young," the bone-identifier remarked. "There's so much left over."

"She was ninety-four," my mother replied.

The bone expert beamed. "Then you've inherited strong bones."

THE DAY OF the funeral, Takahagi wants to show me the robes he has selected for the occasion. Most young priests wear relatively bright colors; Takahagi's otaku brother has agreed to take a break from his Final Fantasy duties to participate in my grandmother's funeral and has already donned the standard bright-yellow-and-cobalt-blue robes that befit a priest under the age of thirty. But Takahagi, that Harajuku devotee, is no ordinary young man. This morning he has chosen a sable-colored robe with a dark gray overgarment. The sable

silk has an iridescent quality to it, sometimes appearing silver, sometimes copper.

"Nice, isn't it?" He holds the robes up in the sunlight.

"Did you special-order that?" I ask.

"There's a guy in Tokyo who makes them for me."

After Takahagi gets dressed, he shows me all of the things he can
do with the overgarment. If you have seen any samurai movies, you
know there is always a scene before battle in which a kimono-wearing
warrior must tie up his sleeves with a rope in order to wield a sword
unencumbered. Takahagi has mastered his priestly robes, which, like
a kimono, also have billowing and potentially troublesome sleeves. He
performs his fashion origami for me, putting the fabric over his head
and tying it behind his back so that his arms can move freely. Then he
unwinds the garment, returning it to its original, constricting position, slips his arm out of a hidden hole, and his arms are free again.

"I'm nervous," he confides. "I've never done a funeral for family
members before."

"Did Takahagi tell you about the Sony funeral?" my otaku cousin
calls out as he plays a round of golf on PlayStation's rendition of
Pebble Beach.

"No," I say.

Takahagi grins. "It was when I was studying to be a priest in Tokyo.
My teacher got a call that someone had died, and he asked me to go
with him to chant sutras. It turned out that we went to the [Sony
chairman] Morita house."

"What was it like?" I ask.

My otaku cousin shakes his head in dismay. "He didn't even look
around."

"I remember that the windows were very big," Takahagi offers. "But
when we went into the main room, I saw the family members, and so
many of them were crying. I had to act completely like a priest."

In the main temple hall, preparations are under way for the funeral.

Enormous bouquets of flowers bearing the names of donors flank the gold Buddha on the altar. My grandfather looks lost in the jungle of oversized lilies and chrysanthemums as he carefully arranges the three urns of bones behind a large bronze incense burner. "Three urns," he boasts to me. "Your grandmother had to have three urns." Once, we would all have been expected to sit on the tatami floor with our feet neatly tucked beneath our thighs. This is a tricky position for many elderly people to assume for long stretches of time; young people, too, have lost the talent for sitting correctly, so Takahagi's father has prepared several rows of folding stools.

During the funeral, Takahagi, in his elegant robes, plays a small gong, while his father ecstatically shouts to my grandmother's soul that she is dead and must leave us. I love the sutra-chanting the most. The priests—Takahagi, his brother, and their father—listen carefully to each other, taking turns to space out each breath so that there is never a break in the sound. Then my mother sings an operatic aria. Now it is my grandfather's turn. He pulls a slip of yellow paper from his pocket and begins to address my grandmother's bones.

He thanks her for taking away his heart murmur when she died. He is feeling much better now. He is sorry that he had to leave her body alone in the house when he went out to dinner, but it really wasn't necessary for her ghost to have locked the doors and windows, making it difficult for him to reenter. He knows that she would like to stay and continue to watch over her children, but it is time for her to leave, and anyway, everyone has attended a prestigious university. Then he begins to cry. The air grows thick, as though the molecules themselves are swollen with emotion.

The weeping is contagious and soon I too am afloat in grief. My grandfather—that hard, hard man—loved my grandmother deeply. It occurs to me now that some of his behavior must have come from the suspicion, if not the actual knowledge, of the photograph of the other man in her purse.

Late in the afternoon, after the funeral and the post-ceremony meal with its troublesome seating arrangement have ended and the guests have gone home, the family sits wilted around a table in the kitchen. I notice that my grandfather is missing.

"I think I know where he is," Takahagi, back in his casual priest clothing, murmurs to me.

We find him alone, perched on a rock by the family burial plot high on top of a hill. It is a gorgeous evening. We are ringed by bamboo and pine trees, and above them the sky is turning pink.

"You know you are really poor when you have no one at home waiting for you," my grandfather says.

"I think," I offer, "I hear a hototogisu singing."

My grandfather tilts his head. "Did you know that the hototogisu migrate here from Taiwan?"

Lately my grandfather has been telling my mother that his happiest years were in Taiwan. He went to university there and stayed on for a time teaching English, before marriage and the war brought him back to Japan. He has even said to me that my love of Japan is something like his love of Taiwan, which I take to mean that he has finally reconciled my half-breed existence with his very traditional family.

"When I die," he says, "I am going to ride a hototogisu back and forth between Japan and Taiwan. When I'm dead, I don't want to ever have to fly in an airplane again."

"You won't have to." Takahagi smiles gently.

"Remember that," my grandfather instructs, "when you come here and a hototogisu is singing. That'll mean I've returned to see you."

That night, as my mother and I lie in our futons, drained by the day, I whisper that it would be cruel not to let my grandfather have his wife's bones.

"That," she says, "is what I've been trying to tell your uncles all along."

It is my grandmother's unexpectedly strong bones and the third urn that solve our burial woes.

The largest urn will stay at the temple, where it will sit under the watchful eye of my cousin until my grandfather is ready to bury it in the temple cemetery.

A second will go home with one of my uncles, who promises to worship the bones every day in his own family shrine. I know that he will quietly take the urn south to Kyushu and bury it with the other *shizoku*, those aristocratic descendents of the samurai who made up my grandmother's family.

My grandfather initially wants my mother to take the Adam's apple back to America, but, thinking quickly, she tells him that it is illegal to import human remains. She suggests that he take the Adam's apple back to his house, and he happily packs it in his small travel bag, which he carries on his lap all the way back to Nagoya.

In the days that follow, he fusses over the small box. He brings it flowers from the garden and sweet bean cakes and fruit from the grocery store. Every morning when I light incense, I find that the little box, bound up in red and gold silk, has been moved from its position of the previous day, as if a mischievous spirit is still struggling to find its place in a new world.

"When he dies," my mother whispers to me late at night, "I'm going to cremate him with that Adam's apple."

Over the next few days, people ask if this is my first Japanese funeral; when I say that it is, they nod and watch me carefully. I have been let in on a secret. When I visit a department store, purveyor of giddy electronics that delight us in the West, I notice specially designed funeral and memorial bento boxes for sale, sans meat. I see men on the bullet train wearing black suits and the telltale black tie; white ties are for weddings. I know where they are headed, what they will be charged with doing. A group of women pass me in Tokyo station carrying a rectangular box whose shape I recognize.

Tradition isn't without some comfort. Once a year during Obon, souls come back to visit for the day. Then graves are swept free of debris, families prepare special foods, and young people dress in summer kimonos and dance together in a circle. I like to imagine that my duty-bound grandmother, though her remains have been divided, will come back to see my grandfather, who will be waiting— and longing—for her.

Uncle Moïse

EDWIDGE DANTICAT

In this piece from PMS poemmemoirstory, *Edwidge Danticat eulogizes her mother's older brother. "I didn't know him as well as my father's brothers, one of whom raised me and about whom I had enough information to write an entire book," she says. She didn't speak at the funeral, feeling that what she wanted to say might not be appropriate for the setting, but, she says, "This was what I wanted to say at Uncle Moïse's funeral so I decided to write it down in this way."*

My uncle Moïse died last week after a six-year battle, first with prostate, then bone cancer. Of all my mother's brothers, Uncle Moïse was my favorite because he often peppered his conversations, whether in English or in Haitian Creole, with the word "Fuck!" Uncle Moïse used different variations of the word freely, even with children (*Speak up, silence is fucked up*), priests (*They can be fucks*), or my very devout and demure parents (*They're your parents, but fuck!*), who could never be swayed by his argument that the most interesting aspect of any language was its cusswords. To substantiate this, he would quote translations of the Marquis de Sade or find interesting uses of the word "fuck" in English-language poetry, his favorite being a verse from a 1971 Philip Larkin poem:

They fuck you up, your mum and dad.
They may not mean to, but they do.

Though I was not fully conscious of the influence of Uncle Moïse's speech pattern on mine, it would surface from time to time in desperate situations. Once, during a heated argument with a boyfriend, I found myself tongue-tied, yet shouting, "You fucking fuck!" then smiling, thinking this was something Uncle Moïse might have said.

A few years into his cancer treatment, Uncle Moïse, who had been both a seminary student and an army officer in Haiti, became an evangelical Christian and began to use a biblical euphemism for the word "fuck." A bad situation became a calamity. When he thought me too quiet, for example, he would now say, "Speak up, silence is a calamity." The switch became a clear sign that Uncle Moïse was taking evangelical Christianity seriously for those of us who had doubted he could. He stopped quoting Sade and Larkin and turned to Bible verses instead, often paraphrasing Deuteronomy 32:35, "Their foot shall slide in time, for the day of calamity is at hand," or Proverbs 6:15, "Therefore shall his calamity come suddenly; suddenly shall he be broken without remedy."

As he grew sicker, Uncle Moïse timed his remaining days in Good Fridays, as if to link his own personal tribulations to the passion of Christ. "I may not have another Good Friday left," he would say, even though he had already seen seventy-one. Good Friday seemed more and more like a perfect day to die in order to be guaranteed a heavenly rebirth. "All Fridays are ultimately good," he would eventually concede, "as long as you're around to see them." (In some parts of Spain, he once explained to me, you ask, "how many Aprils do you have?" to find out someone's age.)

At his wake, speaker after speaker described Uncle Moïse at different periods of his life. People who knew him when he was a Haitian army officer and had to flee the national palace on a motorcycle when his boss, the dictator François "Papa Doc" Duvalier, threatened to have him killed for failing to deliver a letter on time. Others who knew him in connection with his different families (he had been married twice and it was only at his wake that many of his children from his first marriage and his son from the second met one another). While meeting many of his children for the first time myself, I thought of how Uncle Moïse loved to compartmentalize, devoting himself entirely to whatever he was involved with at the time and rarely looking back. Of his long exile from Haiti, which he rarely wanted to discuss, he would only say, "There are enough present calamities so we don't have to keep looking back on past ones." But most of Uncle Moïse's eulogizers had known him as an evangelical Christian at the church where his wake was held and spoke only of his long suffering and, just as he might have wanted, his soul's rebirth in Heaven. During the wake, I kept wishing I could get up and say that what I enjoyed most when in his company was his unfettered use of a four-letter word, but it did not seem appropriate, especially since he had abandoned the word at the end of his life.

The last time I saw Uncle Moïse, against the advice of his doctors, he had driven himself from his home on Long Island to the church in Brooklyn where he was an usher. "It's a calamity sitting around and waiting to die," he had said. Nostalgic, I had thought of his risky cross-county drive as a continuation of his motorcycle flight from certain death and as further evidence of his defiant nature, which neither illness nor the Gospel had completely extinguished. A week later, he was gone.

I cried quite a bit at Uncle Moïse's funeral, mostly because my

mother, his younger sister, was the most inconsolable of his mourners. Exile had scattered her family, she said, and it was only death
that brought us together *en masse* these days. My most sorrowful
moment came, however, on a Friday, three days after the funeral,
when I tried to write Uncle Moïse's name in my computer and
couldn't find on my American keyboard the accent key that would
place the *tréma* over the i in his name. Then exile and loss became
palpable to me. It is the calamity of living and dying in a place where
it takes uncommon effort to spell a fucking name that you have
known your entire life.

The Face of Seung-Hui Cho

WESLEY YANG

In writing about the meaning of the April 2007 shootings at Virginia Tech for n+1, Wesley Yang says, "I found it necessary to go beyond the usual commentary and try to involve the reader in some of the internal turmoil of youth, particularly male youth, and to remind everyone of the aspects of Cho's predicament that are expressed all around us, every day of our lives. . . . The experiment I attempted in this piece—and its success or failure is for others to judge—was to see if I could make that connection."

The first school shooter of the 1990s was an Asian boy who played the violin. I laughed when I heard an account of the rampage from my friend Ethan Gooding, who had survived it. Ethan forgave me my reaction. I think he knew by then that most people, facing up to a real atrocity, as opposed to the hundreds they'd seen on TV, didn't know how to act.

Ethan had left New Providence High School in central New Jersey for the progressive utopia of Simon's Rock College of Bard in

Great Barrington, Massachusetts. Simon's Rock was a school for high school juniors and seniors ready for college-level work, a refuge for brilliant misfits, wounded prodigies, and budding homosexuals. Ethan was a pretty bright kid, brighter than me, but mostly he was a budding homosexual. One day in gym class at New Providence, Ethan made a two-handed set shot from half-court using a kickball while dressed in buttercup-yellow short-shorts and earned the nickname "Maurice." This was not a reference to E. M. Forster's frank novel of gay love, but to Maurice Cheeks, the great Philadelphia 76ers point guard. The unintended resonance was savored by those few of us who could discern it. Ethan had a striking pre-Raphaelite pallor set off against flaming red cheeks and lips with the puckered epicene aspect that speaking the French language too young will impart to a decent American mouth. None of this in itself meant, necessarily, that he was going to become gay, but then—well, he was.

Gay-bashing was less of a hate crime back then and more of a patriotic duty, particularly in a race-segregated, heavily Catholic suburb like New Providence. At Youth & Government, the YMCA-sponsored mock legislature attended by suck-ups with Napoleon complexes, the "governor" from our school introduced a bill to "build an island of garbage off of the Jersey Shore" where we could "put all the homosexuals." We all chortled along, none more loudly than the closet cases in our midst. New Providence was the kind of place you wanted to flee so badly that you trained yourself to forget the impulse.

But then there was a place called New York, only a half hour's drive away. We made our first anxious forays into New York City nightlife, Ethan and I and Jasper Chung, the other Korean kid from my high school (himself a governor of the mock legislature, and also a closet homosexual). We tried to get into the back room of the Limelight, where the real party was happening. "Try to look cute," Ethan told me, brushing my hair with a concerned, appraising look. Then he sucked in his cheeks, which I guess was his way of looking cute, or at least making his face less round. It would be more than a decade and a half before I learned what a smile could do for you (it is one way to hold at bay the world's cruelty), so I made a fish-eyed grimace in emulation of David Gahan of Depeche Mode. They never let us into the back room.

Those were the wild Peter Gatien days, when the place was still bristling with drugs and prostitution, most of which managed to pass us by. But we were assailed by a phalanx of sweaty, shirtless Long Island beefcake. Ethan would, to my frightened astonishment, meet other guys, and go off into a dark corner with them, and leave me to fend for myself, which I was not equipped to do. I'd get dehydrated and wear an anxious scowl. I would attempt some rudimentary sociological and semiotic reading of the scene that swirled all around me. I couldn't relax.

Not that I was myself homosexual. True, my heterosexuality was notional. I wasn't much to look at (skinny, acne-prone, brace-faced, bespectacled, and Asian), and inasmuch as I was ugly, I also had a bad personality. While Ethan was easing himself into same-sex experimentation, I was learning about the torments and transports of misanthropy. "That kid," I remember overhearing one of the baseball players say, "is a misfit." No one ever shoved my head in a locker, the way they did the one amber-tinted Afghani kid, or P. J., the big dumb sweet slow kid, and nobody ever pelted me with rocks, as they did Doug Urbano, who was fat and working class (his father was a truck driver, and sometimes, when he lectured us about the vital role that truck drivers play in the American economy—they really do, you know—he was jeered). But these judgments stayed with me.

Jasper once told me that I was "essentially unlovable." I've always held that observation close to my heart, turning to it often. It's true of some people—that there's no reason anyone should love or care about them, because they aren't appealing on the outside, and that once you dig into the real person beneath the shell (if, for some obscure if not actively perverse reason, you bother), you find the real inner ugliness. I knew lots of people like that—unloved because unlovable. Toward them I was always cold. Maybe I held them at arm's length to disguise from myself our shared predicament. And so, by trying to disguise something from yourself, you declare it to everyone else—because part of what makes a person unlovable is his inability to love.

One day we were hanging out with Ethan in Jasper's room over winter break. Ethan was telling us all about Simon's Rock, and—this might be an invented memory; it feels real, yet I can't rely on it; the very feeling of reality makes me distrust it—Ethan told me that I reminded him of this weird Asian guy at his school, whom he then proceeded to describe. Ethan, cherubic complexion notwithstanding, could actually be pretty mean. He was proud of his ability to wound with a well-chosen phrase coined in an instant, which is not to say that I didn't aspire toward the same facility. It's just that he really had it. In any case, Wayne, my double, was an Asian boy ill at ease in the world and he had a chip on his shoulder. His father had been an officer in the Taiwanese air force, and his mother had been a Suzuki-method violin teacher. For a time, Wayne had been among the best violinists in the world in his age group. He was headed along the familiar track of Asian American assimilation. By the time he arrived at Simon's Rock, he had other things to prove.

The gay guys liked to tease Wayne and intimate that he might secretly be one of them. It was good-natured ribbing, gentle to the extent that it was not tinged with gay malice; and who could begrudge them their share of malice—a little or a lot—given the world they were entering? On top of everything else, an incurable illness spread by the kind of sex you were already having or else aching to have was killing off a whole generation of your predecessors. You could get a rise out of Wayne, and he deserved it: here he was at this place where people were finally free to be who they really were, and who he really was turned out to be someone who didn't want other people to be free to be who they were. He had fled Montana only to discover his continuing allegiance to its mores. And who knows, conceivably he was even a bit bi-curious. "How tough are you?" Wayne's friends used to ask him, egging him on. "I'm tough!" he would shout.

By now the story of Wayne Lo has been well told, though he has not become a figure of American legend. (His certified authentic "murderabilia" drawings were fetching just $7.50 on his website at the time his jailers shut it down.) On Monday, December 14, 1992, a package arrived for him in the mail from a North Carolina company called Classic Arms. It contained two hundred rounds of ammunition that Wayne had ordered using his mother's credit card. The school's dean held the package, and, after questioning Wayne about what was inside it (Wayne assured him that it was a Christmas gift), gave it back to him. Liberals! They'll hand over the ammunition that their enemies will use to kill them.

Ethan told his version of the story to Jasper and me over hamburgers at the A&W Restaurant at the Short Hills Mall. Wayne had started hanging out with some other students who wanted to rebel against the orthodoxy of difference at Simon's Rock. They listened to Rush Limbaugh and joked about killing people. They were suspicious of Jews and blacks and homosexuals and . . . did they make an official exception for Asians? Wayne wrote a paper proposing a solution to the AIDS crisis: Kill them all. He lacked the imagination to come up with the island of garbage disposal. Then, according to psychiatrists hired by his defense, Wayne was overtaken by a "somatic hallucination"—not heard, but directly experienced in his body—of God urging him to punish the sinners of Simon's Rock.

It was a more innocent time, in a way. The Berlin Wall had come down. Crime rates were beginning the historic fall they were to make during the 1990s. American soldiers were ensconced in the Persian Gulf, having recently kept the armies of Saddam Hussein from entering the land of the two holy places. People didn't know about school shooters back then. They still thought that Asian men were happy to be (as Ethan liked to call us) the Other White People. Or even, as many people were suggesting, the New Jews. And for the most part, Asian people were happy—and are. I mean, maybe they were nerds, maybe they were faceless drones, but did anybody know they were angry? What could they be angry about? They were getting rich with the rest of America—and reassuring everyone of our openness and our tolerance for everyone prepared to embrace the American dream.

Lo went around the campus with the Chinese-made SKS carbine rifle that he bought in a neighboring town. He shot and killed two people and wounded four others. Had his rampage not ended prematurely when his rifle repeatedly jammed (cheap Chinese junk), he might have set a record that no one was going to best. Instead, he called the police and negotiated his surrender.

THE PERPETRATOR OF the largest mass murder in American history was an Asian boy who wrote poems, short stories, a novel, and plays. I gazed at the sad blank mug of Seung-Hui Cho staring out at the world on CNN.com—the face-forward shot that was all the press had before they received Cho's multimedia manifesto, mailed on the day of the shootings, with its ghastly autoerotic glamour shots (Cho pointing gun at camera; Cho with a hammer; Cho pointing gun at his head). I felt, looking at the photo, a very personal revulsion. Millions of others reviled this person, but my own loathing was more intimate. Those lugubrious eyes, that elongated face behind wire-frame glasses: *He looks like me*, I thought.

This was another inappropriate reaction. But the photo leapt out at me at a funny time in my life. I had come to New York five years earlier, to create a life for myself there. I had not created a life for myself there. I had wanted to find the emerging writers and thinkers of my generation. I had found the sycophants, careerists, and media parasites who were redefining mediocrity for the twenty-first century. I had wanted to remain true to myself as a writer, and also to succeed; I wanted to be courageous and merciless in defense of the downtrodden, and I wanted to be celebrated for it. This was a naive and puerile desire and one that could not be realized—at least not by me, not in this world. It could not be done without a facility (and a taste) for ingratiation that I lacked. It could not be done without first occupying a position of strength and privilege that I did not command—because, as Jesus said, to him who hath, more will be given; nor without being enterprising and calculating in a way that I wasn't—because, as Jesus went on to say, to him who hath not, even that which he hath will be taken from him. It seemed to me that every kind of life, and even the extinction of life, was preferable to the one that I was living, which is not to say I had the strength either to change my life, or to end it.

And then to be confronted by that face. Because physiognomy is a powerful thing. It establishes identification and aversion, and all the more so in an age that is officially color-blind. Such impulses operate beneath the gaze of the supervisory intelligence, at a visceral level that may be the most honest part of us. You see a face that looks like yours. You know that there's an existential knowledge you have in common with that face. Both of you know what it's like to have a cultural code superimposed atop your face, and if it's a code that abashes, nullifies, and unmans you, then you confront every visible reflection of that code with a feeling of mingled curiosity and wariness. When I'm out by myself in the city—at the movies or at a restaurant—I'll often see other Asian men out by themselves in the city. We can't even look at each other for the strange vertigo we induce in one another.

Let's talk about legible faces. You know those short, brown-toned South American immigrants that pick your fruit, slaughter your meat, and bus your tables? Would you—a respectable person with a middle-class upbringing—ever consider going on a date with one of them? It's a rude question, because it affects to inquire into what everyone gets to know at the cost of forever leaving it unspoken. But if you were to put your unspoken thoughts into words, they might sound something like this: Not only are these people busing the tables, slaughtering the meat, and picking the fruit, they are the descendants of the people who bused the tables, slaughtered the meat, and picked the fruit of the Aztecs and Incas. The Spanish colonizers slaughtered or mixed their blood with the princes, priests, scholars, artisans, warriors, and beautiful women of the indigenous Americas, leaving untouched a class of Morlocks bred for good-natured servility and thus now tailor-made to the demands of an increasingly feudal postindustrial America. That's, by the way, part of the emotional undertow of the immigration debate, the thing that makes an honest appraisal of the issue impossible, because you can never put anything right without first admitting you're in the wrong.

So: Seung-Hui Cho's face. A perfectly unremarkable Korean face—beady-eyed, brown-toned, a small plump-lipped mouth, eyebrows high off his eyelids, with crooked glasses perched on his nose. It's not an ugly face, exactly; it's not a badly made face. It's just a face that has nothing to do with the desires of women in this country. It's a face belonging to a person who, if he were e-mailing you, or sending you instant messages, and you were a normal, happy, healthy American girl at an upper second-tier American university—and that's what Cho was doing in the fall of 2005, e-mailing and writing instant messages to girls—you would consider reporting to campus security. Which is what they did, the girls who were contacted by Cho.

FIRST, YOU IMAGINE, they tried to dissuade him in the usual way. You try to be polite, but also to suggest that you'd actually prefer that your correspondent, if he could, you know, maybe—oh, I don't know—*Disappear from your life forever? How about that?*—and you had to do this subtly enough not to implicate yourself in anything damaging to your own self-image as a nice person, but then not so subtly that your correspondent would miss the point. When Cho missed the point, the girls had to call the campus police. They did not want him arrested, and they did not press charges. They just had to make clear that while Cho thought he was having one kind of encounter (a potentially romantic one), he was in fact having another kind of encounter (a potentially criminal one), and to show him that the state would intervene on their behalf if he couldn't come to terms with this reality. And so, the police didn't press any charges, but they did have a man-to-man talk with Cho, and conveyed to him the message that it would be better if he cut it out.

Seung-Hui Cho's is the kind of face for which the appropriate response to an expression of longing or need involves armed guards. I am not questioning the choices that these girls made; I am affirming those choices. But I'm talking about the Cho that existed before anyone was killed by him—the one who showed proficiency in beer pong at the one fraternity party his roommates took him to, and who told his roommates he had a girlfriend named Jelly who was a supermodel from outer space; who called one of his roommates to tell him that he had been on vacation with Vladimir Putin; and who e-mailed Lucinda Roy, director of the creative writing program, seeking guidance about how to submit his novel to publishers. "My novel is relatively short," he wrote. "It's sort of like Tom Sawyer, except that it's really silly or pathetic, depending on how you look at it."

Of course, there are a lot of things that Cho might have done to change his social fortunes that he declined to do. Either out of incompetence, stubbornness, or plain old bat-shit craziness, Cho missed many boats that might have ferried him away from his dark fate. For one, he could have dressed a little bit better. He might have tried to do something with his hair. Being a little less bat-shit crazy couldn't have hurt. Above all, he could have cultivated his taste in music. He was "obsessed with downloading music from the Internet," the press reported, putting a sinister cast on something that everyone of a certain age does. But the song he continually played on his laptop, driving his roommates to distraction, wasn't some nihilistic rhapsody of wasted youth. It wasn't Trent Reznor of Nine Inch Nails saying he wanted to fuck you like an animal, and it wasn't the thick lugubrious whine of James Hetfield of Metallica declaring that what he'd felt, and what he'd known, never shone through in what he'd shown.

No, it was the cruddiest, most generic grunge-rock anthem of the '90s, Collective Soul's "Shine." "Shine" came out in 1994, and you only had to hear the first minute to know that whatever was truly unyielding about the music Nirvana spawned by breaking punk into the mainstream was already finished. The song cynically mouths "life-affirming" cliches noxious to the spirit of punk rock, but then these are not, given the situation, without their own pathos. You could picture the Cho who stalked around campus not saying a word to anyone, even when a classmate offered him money to speak, coming home in silence to listen to these lyrics repeat in an infinite loop on his laptop, and even, one day, to write them on his wall. The song implores some person or higher power to teach the singer to speak and share; to direct him where to go; and to affirm the existence of love at that destination. It seeks evidence of an unseen and saving power:

Whoa-oh-oh-oh, heaven let your light shine down.

"You were the single biggest dork school shooter of all time," opined one Internet chat board participant, and it was hard to disagree. Cho was so disaffected that he couldn't even get the symbols of disaffection right. In the fall of 2005, when he made the mistake of instant-messaging girls, Cho was also attending Nikki Giovanni's large creative writing class. He wore reflector glasses with a baseball cap obscuring his face. Giovanni, who believed that openness was vital to the goals of the class, stood by his desk at the beginning of each session to make him take off the disguise. He later began showing up with a scarf wrapped around his head, "Bedouin style," as Giovanni put it. When the attendance sheet was passed around, he signed his name as a question mark.

The class set Cho off, somehow—maybe because he had enrolled in the hope that his genius would be recognized, and it was not recognized. He began snapping pictures of female classmates with his cell-phone camera from underneath his desk. Eventually, many of the seventy students enrolled in the class stopped coming. That's when Giovanni went to Lucinda Roy and insisted that Cho be barred from her workshop. She refused, in the words of one article about it, to be "bullied" by Cho.

"He was writing, just weird things," Giovanni told the *New York Times*. "I don't know if I'm allowed to say what he was writing about. . . . He was writing poetry, it was terrible, it was not like poetry, it was intimidating."

Giovanni's personal website has a list of all her honors and awards and another page for all the honorary degrees she has earned—nineteen since 1972—and a brief biography that identifies her as "a world-renowned poet, writer, commentator, activist, and educator," whose "outspokenness, in her writing and in lectures, has brought the eyes of the world upon her." Oprah Winfrey has named her one of her twenty-five living legends. "We are sad today, and we will be sad for quite a while," the sixty-three-year-old eminence told the convocation to mourn Seung-Hui Cho's victims. "We are not moving on, we are embracing our mourning."

It's a perfectly consistent picture: Giovanni the winner of awards, and Giovanni the wise and grandmotherly presence on *Oprah*. But if you knew more about the writing of Nikki Giovanni, you couldn't help but wonder two things. What would the Nikki Giovanni of 2007 have made of a poem published by the Nikki Giovanni of 1968, and what would the Nikki Giovanni of 1968 have made of the Nikki Giovanni of the present? The Nikki Giovanni of 1968 wrote this:

Nigger
Can you kill
Can you kill
Can a nigger kill
Can a nigger kill a honkie
Can a nigger kill the Man
Can you kill nigger
Huh? nigger can you
kill
Do you know how to draw blood
Can you poison
Can you stab-a-Jew
Can you kill huh? nigger
Can you kill

Back then Giovanni was writing about a race war that seemed like it really might break out at home, even as the country was fighting what she saw as an imperialist war in Vietnam. Black militancy was something that many people admired, and many more felt sympathy toward, given the brutal history of enslavement, rape, terrorism, disenfranchisement, lynching, and segregation that blacks had endured in this country. And so you wonder what would have happened if, for instance, Cho's poems (and thoughts) had found a way to connect his pain to his ethnic identity. Would Giovanni have been less intimidated if she could have understood Cho as an aggrieved Asian man, instead of an aggrieved man who happened to be Asian? Or if he were black and wrote the way he did? Or if he were Palestinian and managed to tie his violent grievances to a real political conflict existing in the world? (Can you bomb-a-Jew?) Giovanni knows black rage, and she knows the source of women's bitterness. We all do. We know gay pride. We know, in short, identity politics, which, when it isn't acting as a violent outlet for the narcissism of the age, can serve as its antidote, binding people into imagined collectivities capable of taking action to secure their interests and assert their personhood.

Cho did not think of himself as Asian; he did not think of himself ethnically at all. He was a pimply friendless suburban teenager whom no woman would want to have sex with: that's what he was. And it turned out that in his own imagination he was a warrior on behalf of every lonely invisible human being in America. This was his ghastly, insane mistake. This is what we learned from the speech that Cho gave in the video he mailed to NBC news. For Cho, the cause to fight for is "the dorky kid that [you] publicly humiliated and spat on," whom you treated like "a filthy street dog" and an "ugly, little, retarded, low-life kid"—not just Cho, not just his solitary narcissistic frenzy, but also that of his "children," his "brothers and sisters"—an imagined community of losers who would leave behind their status as outcasts from the American consensus and attain the dignity of warriors—by killing innocent civilians.

Cho enclosed his speech, too, in the NBC packet, as "writings."

You had every thing you wanted.
Your Mercedes wasn't enough,
you brats,
your golden necklaces weren't enough,
you snobs,
your trust fund wasn't enough . . .

You have vandalized my heart,
raped my soul
and torched my conscience.
You thought it was one pathetic, bored life you were
    extinguishing.

I die like Jesus Christ,
    to inspire generations of the weak and defenseless people.

Cho imagines the one thing that can never exist—the coming to consciousness and the joining in solidarity of the modern class of losers. Though his soft Asian face could only have been a hindrance to him, Cho did not perceive his pain as stemming from being Asian: he did not perceive himself in a world of identity politics, of groups and fragments of groups, of groups oppressing and fighting other groups. Cho's world is a world of individually determined fortunes, of winners and losers in the marketplace of status, cash, and expression. Cho sees a system of social competition that renders some people absolutely immiserated while others grow obscenely rich.

When I was at Rutgers I knew a guy named Samuel. He was prematurely middle-aged, not just in his dimensions, which were bloated, and not just in his complexion, which was pale but flushed with the exertion of holding himself upright—sweat would dapple the groove between his upper lip and nose—but above all in something he exuded, which was a pheromone of loneliness and hostility. Samuel had gone off to Reed College, and, after a couple of years of feeling alienated in that liberal utopia, he had returned east. Samuel was one of the students at Rutgers who was clearly more intellectually sophisticated than I. He knew more, he had read more, and it showed. He was the kind of nominal left-winger who admired the works of

Carl Schmitt before many others had gotten onto that trend, and he knew all about the Frankfurt School, and he was already jaded about the postmodernists when others were still enraptured by the discovery of them. In addition to being the kind of leftist who read a Nazi legal theorist to be contrarian, Samuel was also the kind of aspiring academic so contemptuous of the postmodern academy that he was likely to go into investment banking and make pots of money while jeering at the rest of humanity, because that was so much more punk rock than any other alternative to it. He identified his "lifestyle"—and of course he put that word into derisive quote marks when he used it—as "indie rock," but Samuel's irony had extra bite to it, real cruelty and rancor, that was tonally off-kilter for the indie rock scene, which, as it manifested itself at Rutgers, was taciturn to the point of autism, passive-aggressive, and anti-intellectual, but far too cool and subdued for the exertions of overt cruelty.

You saw a look of sadness and yearning in Samuel's face when he had subsided from one of his misanthropic tirades—there was no limit to the scorn he heaped on the intellectual pretensions of others—and it put you on guard against him. What you sensed about him was that his abiding rage was closely linked to the fact that he was fat and ugly in a uniquely unappealing way, and that this compounded with his unappealing rage made him the sort of person that no woman would ever want to touch. He seemed arrayed in that wild rancor that sexual frustration can bestow on a man, and everything about his persona—his coruscating irony, his unbelievable intellectual snobbery—seemed a way to channel and thus defend himself against this consuming bitterness. He was ugly on the outside and once you got past that you found the true ugliness on the inside.

And then below that ugliness you found a vulnerable person who desperately needed to be seen and touched and known as a human phenomenon. And above all, you wanted nothing to do with that, because once you touched the source of his loneliness, there would be no end to it, and even if you took it upon yourself to appease this unappeasable need, he would eventually decide to revenge himself against a world that had held him at bay, and there would be no better target for this revenge than you, precisely because you were the person who'd dared to draw the nearest. This is what you felt instantly, without having to put it into words (it's what I felt anyway, though it might have been pure projection), the moment you met Samuel. For all that he could be amusing to talk to, and for all that he was visibly a nice guy despite all I've just said, you were careful to keep your distance.

Samuel used to complain about declining academic standards. He said that without much work he was acing all of his classes. This was a way of exalting himself slightly while mostly denigrating others, which made it an exemplary statement of his, but it was also a suspect statement, since no one had asked. One day, while I was in the history department's front office, I noticed a plastic crate full of hanging folders. In one of those folders, I found my own academic transcript in its entirety. Then I looked for Samuel's, and found it. His transcript, like mine, was riddled with Ds and Fs. And while what Samuel had said about academic standards and his own aptitude was surely true, it was also true that he had lied—and I suppose I understand why. If your only claim to self-respect was your intellectual superiority, and you had more or less flunked out of Reed College because of the crushing loneliness and depression you encountered once you realized that liberal utopia wasn't going to embrace you as it did the willowy, stylish high school outcasts who surrounded you—and if your grades weren't much better at Rutgers (a pathetic public university, even though you hated Reed more), you might be forced to lie about those grades, because they were the public face of all you had left—your intellectual superiority—and even after all you'd endured, or maybe because of it, your public face still mattered. Unaware that the contrary evidence was there for anyone to check (it should not have been) or that a person inclined to check it existed (I should not have looked), you would assume that you could tell this lie without being caught.

I mentioned this incident to a mutual acquaintance, who proceeded to tell Samuel, who accused me of making up lies about him, and turned me into the great enemy of his life—he was clearly looking for one—which was too bad and a little disconcerting, because, as I explained to him, he and his grades had never meant anything to me. And yet I had only read two transcripts, his and mine, mostly because I suspected, correctly, that he was telling lies. Samuel had been wronged by me, and it would have been right for me to apologize, but I had some hostility of my own, so instead I told him that he was ugly on the outside, but even uglier on the inside, and that he meant nothing to me, and his enmity counted for nothing to me. And this was true. I had recognized him as a person with whom I had some mutual understanding—overlapping interests and, most of all, overlapping pretensions—but I never wanted him as a friend. The image this whole affair calls up is the scene in *Born on the Fourth of July* in which two paraplegics in wheelchairs start wrestling around in anger, and then tip each other into a ditch by the side of the road, and fall out of their wheelchairs, and roll around on the ground in the dirt, from which they are unable to lift themselves.

I saw Samuel at a coffee shop near Union Square about a year ago. He was chatting up the Eastern European counter girls. You could tell that he was a regular. He had put on a lot of weight and lost more of his hair, and his skin had lost none of its sebaceous excess. He had really become, at thirty-two or thirty-three, the ruined middle-aged man that he already seemed on the cusp of becoming in youth. He seemed like a nice, harmless guy, but then you could still discern loneliness and sexual desperation clinging to him, though it had lost some of its virulence. I was glad to see his resignation. And I knew that he was probably very rich, and I felt weirdly good on his behalf to know that if he had to be lonely, if he had to be one of the millions of sexually null men in America—and for all I knew, he could have studied the Game and become a world-class seducer in the intervening years, though it seemed unlikely ("Hey guys—quick question for you—do you believe in magic spells?"—I couldn't see it)—at least he could be rich.

Lack of money had taught me the value of money. I had learned that when I didn't have it—and by this I mean, really having none of it, as in, like, nothing, which was most of the time—I would become extremely unhappy. And that when I did have it, even a little bit of it, which was rare, my despondency was assuaged, and I became like a dry and dwindling houseplant that would rally and surge up from out of its dolor when watered. I deduced from this pattern that what I needed to do was find an occupation that would pay me a salary—it was amazing to think how long I had gone without one—and then I would have money all the time, and then I would be, if not happy, at least OK. And to come to this realization seemed a little bit like the moment in *1984* when Winston Smith decides that he loves Big Brother, but then even more than that it just felt like growing up and it felt like life. And so I figured that Samuel was fine; and while I was very far from fine, I thought someday I'd catch on to something and I'd eventually be fine too.

And maybe I still will, at that.

A FRIEND OF mine wrote a book about online dating. She talked to hundreds of people about their experiences. Online, you become the person you've always known yourself to be, deep down. Online, you're explicit about the fact that you are paying for a service, and you're explicit about the fact that what you're paying for is to get what you really want, and what you're paying for is the ability to remove that annoying bit of residual romantic nonsense that gets us into annoying situations in life where we have to face up to the fact that we are rational profit maximizers in nothing so much as those intimate areas where we pretend to be otherwise. And so, people on the dating sites disclose what they really want, and also what they really don't want.

This friend talked to one man from Maryland who put up his profile on Match.com one night a few years back. This man had good reason to think he would do well on the site. He made more than $150,000 a year; he was white; he was over six feet tall. The next morning, he woke up and checked his account. Over the course of the previous night, he had gotten many responses. How many responses had he gotten? How well could he expect to do, being a man able to check off, without lying, boxes that certified that he made more than $150,000 a year, that he was six feet four inches tall, and that he was white? How well do you think he was going to do on that site where people disclosed what they really wanted out of life and also what they really didn't want?

He had gotten six thousand responses in one night. The fact was that if there was something intriguing or beautiful about that man—and there's something beautiful about us all, if you look deeply enough—someone was going to take the trouble to find it out, and they'd love him for that thing, not because he was six foot four inches tall, and not because he made more than $150,000 a year. You'd find out about his love of truth and poetry, to the extent that it existed, or at least his ability to make you laugh, or his own ability to laugh at things that made you laugh too—things on TV. You could watch TV together. Because the thing you wanted to do was to find true love and have that true love coincide with everything else that you wanted from life, so that you could have all the benefits of one kind of ease, and all the moral credit that others had to win by forgoing that kind of ease (but you could have it all, so why not?), and so you were going to put yourself in a position to do that. And you weren't going to answer the ads of anyone with beady lugubrious eyes in a forlorn, brown-tinted face, and if that person wrote you a message, you weren't going to write him back, and you'd probably even, if it seemed like it was necessary, block all further e-mails from that person. And you'd be right to do that. You'd be behaving in the way that any rational person in your situation would behave. We all agree that the rational thing to do is to shut every trace of that person's existence out of your view. The question, though, is—what if it's not you shutting out the losers? What if you're the loser whom everyone is shutting out? Of course, every loser is shutting out an even more wretched loser. But what if, as far as you know, you're the lowest person at the lowest end of this hierarchy? What is your rational move then?

You wake to find yourself one of the disadvantaged of the fully liberated sexual marketplace. If you are a woman, maybe you notice that men have a habit of using and discarding you, pleading their own inconstancy and premature emotional debauchery as a sop to your wounded feelings. If you are a man, maybe you notice that the women who have been used and discarded by other, more highly valued men are happy to restore (for a while) their own broken self-esteem by stepping on you while you are prone, and reminding you that even a society of outcasts has its hierarchies. Indeed, these hierarchies are policed all the more ruthlessly the closer to the bottom you go.

For these people, we have nothing but options. Therapy, selective serotonin reuptake inhibitors, alcoholism, drug addiction, pornography, training in mixed martial arts, mail-order brides from former Soviet republics, sex tours in Southeast Asia, prostitution, videogame consoles, protein shakes and weightlifting regimens, New Age medicine, obsession with pets or home furnishings, the recovery movement—all of which are modes of survival as opposed to forms of life. Each of these options compensates for a thing, love, that no person can flourish without, and each, in a different way, offers an endlessly deferred resolution to a conundrum that is effectively irresolvable. You could even say that our culture feeds off the plight of the poor in spirit in order to create new dependencies. You might even dare to say that an undernourished human soul—desperate and flailing, prone to seeking voluntary slavery in the midst of freedom and prosperity—is so conducive to the creation of new markets that it is itself the indispensable product of our culture and our time, at once its precondition and its goal.

THERE'S A FAMILIAR narrative we all know about high school losers. It's the narrative of smart sitcoms and even edgy indie films. The high school loser grows up, fills out, goes to Brown or RISD, and becomes the ideal guy for every smart, sensitive, quirky-but-cute girl with glasses (who is, in turn, the female version of the loser made good). The traits that hindered him (or her) in one phase of life turn out to be a blessing in another, more enlightened phase, or else get cast aside. For many people, this is an accurate description of their experience—it is the experience of the writers and producers of these stories.

In the indie film version of Seung-Hui Cho's life, the escort Cho hired a few weeks before his massacre wouldn't have danced for him for fifteen minutes in a motel room and then shoved him away when he tried to touch her. Not every one of the girls he tried to talk to would have recoiled in horror from him. Something would have happened in that film to remind him, and us, of his incipient humanity—that horribly menaced and misshapen thing. He would have found a good-hearted person who had perhaps been touched in some way by the same hysteria—and don't we all know something about it?—that had consumed Cho's soul. And this good-hearted girl or boy would have known how to forgive Cho for what he couldn't forgive himself—the unbearable, all-consuming shame of being ugly, weak, sick, poor, clumsy, and ungifted.

We know that Cho had dreamt of this indie film ending. He had been dreaming of it for a long time. In the spring semester of 2006, he wrote a story about a boy estranged from his classmates: "Everyone is smiling and laughing as if they're in heaven-on-earth, something magical and enchanting about all the people's intrinsic nature that Bud will never experience." But eventually the boy meets a "Gothic Girl," to whom he breaks down and confesses, "I'm nothing. I'm a loser. I can't do anything. I was going to kill every god damn person in this damn school, swear to god I was, but I . . . couldn't. I just couldn't."

Cho's short story about the Gothic Girl should have ended, but did not, with this declaration. Instead, he and the girl steal a car and drive to her house, where she retrieves "a .8 caliber automatic rifle and a M16 machine gun," and the story concludes when she tells the narrator, "You and me. We can fight to claim our deserving throne."

In real life, there was no Gothic Girl, no me to Cho's you, no other willing actors—whether sympathetic, heroic, or equally violently deranged—to populate the self-made movie of his life.

Having failed to make it as a novelist—he really did send a book proposal to a New York publisher—Cho decided to make a film. This was a familiar trajectory, with a twist. He was going to collaborate with all the major television networks on it. In the days before his date with a self-appointed destiny, Cho was spotted working out in the college gym. He wanted his scrawny arms and chest to appear more credibly menacing than they were. How many of those men working their arms to the point of exhaustion were driven by the vain notion that they could improve their sexual prospects in the process? Cho had no such illusions. He was preparing a spectacle for the world to witness on TV, and he needed to look the part.

The Poet's Mother's
Deathbed Conversion

JEFFREYETHANLEE.BLOGSPOT.COM

My mom was in her hospital bed, smiling with rare warmth. The whiteness of the room was intense under the fluorescent lights. Maybe she was glad because I was the only one in our family to go to see her.

Without me saying anything, she said, "Go ahead, be happy."

"What are you talking about?" I asked.

"I want you to just be happy."

Seeing my puzzled expression, she finally said, "You can write poetry."

I was shocked, and she kept smiling. This was the same person who was so hell-bent on me being in science, math, or law. The same person who had said, "Poetry is garbage. Why do you want to add more garbage to the garbage of all the lousy people of the world?"

I was shocked but hoping to believe it, after all. This time she could be dead in the near future. Maybe this was her deathbed conversion into a supportive mom. She didn't have much else to say, and neither did I.

I felt like a terrible dark cloud had been lifted off my head.

I wondered as I drove away if I hadn't misjudged her all my life.

But then a few weeks later the specialists sorted it out, and it wasn't advanced liver cancer. It wasn't any kind of cancer. It was just an anomaly.

So she was out and feeling strong again like her old self at home, in her kitchen.

Then she told me, "You know what I said in the hospital?"

"Yes," I smiled. This was one of the few truly happy memories I had of her.

"Well, forget it. I only said that because I thought I was dying."

The Storyteller

PLANETMEXICALI.SQUARESPACE.COM

My neighbor in Mexicali told me this one. We live at the end of a dead-end street in an old but quiet area of the city. Our red-tile-roofed, low-built adobe houses share a single wall. I was out in front of my garden sweeping sand and eucalyptus leaves off the sidewalk, and Cuate was a few feet away leaning against the bed of my Dodge truck and drinking a Tecate. The both of us were awash in the white glare of noonday sun.

Only a few years back, he told me, a Hollywood production company had come to town to begin prepping for a new action thriller starring Sean Penn, Brad Pitt, or Mike Douglas. Cuate couldn't remember which, but what he did remember is that an ad had been placed in the local newspaper, *La Voz,* calling for auditions, and Mexicanos, young and old, skinny and fat, negros and guerros alike, were coming from as far away as Algodones and Ensenada for their one fleeting chance at stardom. As I swept I listened. That's quite a story, I thought. I pictured the long line of hopeful would-be extras, snaking through a parking lot and down the street. It's not every day that someone like Brawd Peete comes to your puebla.

Cuate has long black hair, a paintbrush mustache, and a face like a hatchet. He is so emaciated from years of drinking that his faded blue jeans and plaid workshirt hang on him like a windblown plastic bag stuck on a tree branch. He is not the most sophisticated or educated person I know. He's lived in the same house all his life and has raked leaves for a living for the past twenty-five years, but I'll tell you what, he's far more advanced at telling a story than I could ever dream of being. He's practiced at it. With each sip of his beer and each new twist to his tale, his face glows, and broken blood vessels dot his complexion like violet stars across a copper sky. He's a born thespian.

It's obvious where his passion for stories comes from. His mother, Fernanda, who happened to be sitting in front of their kitchen door, is pure Yaqui from Obregon, Sonora. She's over in her robe with her hair up in curlers, smoking a Marlboro and bent forward with a flyswatter smashing a never-ending line of red ants passing through my garden and in front of her house. According to her culture's storied tradition, her grandmother had passed on to her mother mystical star-crossed stories about powerful curanderas and magical saints, and just as her mother did for her, Fernanda is doing her best to pass on the tradition to the next generation.

Sometimes when she sees me come home from work, she invites me over to sit in front of their house with the family and exchange stories. The air is always heavy with the aroma of lard and beans. Stray dogs roam the front yard, and everyone's got a beer in hand while she tells us about an aunt she had who could cure cancer with a little saliva and dust; strange, inexplicable tales about dead girls selling popcorn in the cinema; and Nazi polka parties erupting in hidden villages of the Sierra Madre.

My Spanish isn't all there yet, but whenever I stumble on a word or a phrase, or take a moment to ponder any subtext to their tales, they wait for me. I'm telling you, they have this way of pulling you in. There is something so honest and pure about the way they tell stories. It's like they convince you that they can see it, can feel it, pulse inside their hearts. And they want you to feel the same beat.

The time Fernanda told me about the dead girl in the cinema, she explained to me that on a night she went with friends to see a Pedro Infante movie, she had gone off by herself to the concession counter to buy popcorn, where she got into a conversation with one of her classmates, Iliana, who worked behind the counter.

Apparently Iliana had to leave her sister's quinceanera party early to report to work. Pobrecita, Fernanda had said; this girl had her hair curled tightly into a bun in back, and then redirected upwards and forwards into a French twist. Fernanda emphasized these details, because when she had gone back to her friends with the popcorn, she remembered telling everyone how beautiful Iliana looked.

It wasn't until the next day that Cuate's mother read in *La Voz* about how Iliana's parents had arranged for an older brother to take her to work in the family car. They never made it to the movie theatre. Paco, handsome and elegant in a blue tuxedo, was way too drunk to drive. He swerved into oncoming traffic on Avenida Reforma and took on a camionetta head-on. Both brother and sister died on impact. Witnesses stated that the bus flattened their car like a tortilla.

And I'm thinking, yeah, yeah, yeah. I know that as Fernanda is telling this story the entire family must be watching to see my reaction. I realize that she couldn't have seen her friend at the theatre because Iliana had never made it, and I'm trying not to look at my watch or show any signs of disbelief, when suddenly I hear the voice of Cuate's mother trail off in dismay. Suddenly her words seem softer, and I begin to sense a distance developing between us like the deeper she gets into her story, the farther away she drifts. I can begin to hear in the distance the sounds of cars on a nearby street. Dogs barking. Kids laughing, and when I look up, I see Cuate's mother looking straight at me with a tear sliding down her cheek. I remember looking at the texture of her skin, how it was withered and cracked like the side of an adobe wall. I realize that there is a truth in her words that I will never know.

Silence. A dramatic pause.

When I look up, I see that she's not looking at me at all. All of her attention is on her hand, which she has fanned out along the front of her shoulder. As she finishes her story, she's passing it along the collar of her robe as if she's trying to wipe butter off her fingertips.

Lavish Dwarf Entertainment

ALICE DREGER

Alice Dreger sometimes fantasizes about writing novels: "Fiction would be so much easier," she says. "No research necessary, and I could, at will, switch personalities and bodies, events and imaginings, low places and climaxes. I'd be omnipotent, omniscient, omnipresent." This story about dwarfism appeared in the Bioethics Forum, *an online offshoot of the* Hastings Center Report, *a journal dedicated to ethical issues in medicine and the life sciences.*

A dwarf walks into a bar.

I was searching for a funny anecdote that would begin with that sentence when I ran into Danny Black, a dwarf who has walked into a lot of bars. At the time, I was writing a book about conjoined twins and had decided to open with amusing bar stories from people born with body types that mess with ideas of normal.

So I asked an acquaintance with a positive reputation in the dwarfism community to post an inquiry from me on one of the online lists.

Danny answered, in part to exclaim that, hey, we live in the same town, we should meet up. I looked at his e-mail address and realized that I'd seen his car around my neighborhood. It's hard to miss. It's a white 1989 Honda Accord emblazoned with a bunch of corporate endorsements and, in the biggest font possible, the name of his company: Shortdwarf.com.

Turns out Danny's the kind of dwarf that gets paid to walk into a bar—as Cupid on Valentine's Day, as Santa's elf just before Christmas, as a leprechaun on St. Patrick's Day. He also does private parties, including children's birthday parties (he ties a mean poodle balloon), bachelorette parties (he strips down to boxers while teasing the bride), and the like. For adult birthday parties, he's got a very funny doctor routine involving an enema bag. Danny's company also manages other dwarf talent nationwide. In deference to his critics, Danny calls himself the Heidi Fleiss of dwarf entertainment.

The gig for which he's become somewhat famous was the 2003 Miami bachelor party of Thomas Bruderman, who was, back then, a darling trader for Fidelity. Bruderman was marrying the daughter of now-defamed Tyco head Dennis Kozlowski. The story about Danny's involvement in the bachelor party broke on the front page of the *Wall Street Journal*:

> The fun included a stay at the ritzy Delano Hotel for some, a yacht cruise and entertainment by at least one dwarf hired for the occasion. "Some people are just into lavish dwarf entertainment," says the 4-foot-2 Danny Black, a part-owner of Shortdwarf.com, an outfit that rents dwarfs for parties starting at $149 an hour.

That story won't die. The feds have ended up conducting an investigation into whether the party and similar events represented a misuse of investors' money, and, four years after the event, Danny's still getting calls from reporters interested in unusual Wall Street business practices. Lobster is apparently one thing, a rented dwarf is another.

At the time I met Danny, I couldn't understand why anyone would go out of his or her way to hire a dwarf entertainer, though I did quickly come to understand why Danny did the work. When there's work, it pays well. He doesn't make a fortune—he rents his apartment, and his car's odometer reads 390,000 miles and counting—but it's a living. I remember that when he got back from Miami in 2003 he told me about the crazy money flying around, some of it into his hands. He also really likes doing entertainment work. I know it sounds corny, but Danny likes to make people laugh. And he's good at it. And it feels good to do work you're good at. His stock saying is this: "Why shouldn't I use my disadvantage to my advantage?" Height-plus-talent: it's a well-known money-making formula in professional basketball, modeling, and politics.

Still, much as I liked Danny from the start, and though I quickly came to see him as a good friend, it was hard to reconcile my life's work with his. Mine has been about getting people past anatomical stereotypes—past the idea that you can mark people off as different simply because they're conjoined, or really short, or physically between the sexes. His work seemed to be about making money off of those very stereotypes.

THE LEADING SUPPORT and advocacy organization for people with dwarfism, Little People of America (LPA), was started by the dwarf actor Billy Barty as a publicity stunt for the city of Reno, Nevada. The idea was to get all these very short folks together for a weekend in Reno, "the biggest little city in the world," so that the national press might sit up and take notice of the town. As often happens when you get together people who have in common a stigmatized identity, a peer support group spontaneously coalesced. For years, the group was informal, mostly centered around happy socializing. Bit by bit, over the years, the members started sharing information about employment opportunities, about medical treatments for the physical problems associated with some kinds of dwarfism, about specialized products like portable step stools. But they kept taking time just to socialize, too. Everyone who goes to an LPA convention tells me the same thing: you go to LPA and get useful information, sure, but you also go to play cards and knock back a few and meet potential mates.

Although a number of the early members of LPA were entertainers —like Billy Barty then and Danny Black today—it didn't take long for LPA to celebrate a very different ideal: the fully assimilated dwarf. The icon of this was Lee Kitchens (1930–2003). The bio of Kitchens in Betty Adelson's book, *The Lives of Dwarfs*, sums it up this way: "Lee Kitchens: Engineer, Inventor, Role Model." Indeed, Kitchens's professional career would have made any parent proud: white-collar engineer, university lecturer, corporate executive, mayor of his town. The picture of Kitchens and his family in Adelson's book looks like a promo shot for "Leave It to Beaver," except that mom, dad, daughter, and son all appear to be dwarfs. (As it turns out, the son grew to five feet seven inches.) Kitchens's stereotype-breaking life showed that people with dwarfism could get good educations, good jobs, live in nice houses—and stay out of entertainment. Parents of children with dwarfism didn't have to fear that their children would have the options of sideshows or nothing.

Danny used to attend the LPA conventions in part to sell the specialized products he markets to people living with short bodies and short limbs. His bottom wiper has been a best-seller; he sells them mostly to fellow dwarfs, but sometimes also online to very fat and very buff people and folks with other kinds of movement impairments. But, of the money Danny earned through the convention, most of it came from the sale of his dwarf-themed T-shirts. A popular one reads simply "short happens." Over time, these shirts got increasingly in-your-face. The young folks at LPA were partial to "Go ahead, call me a midget. I can use another felony conviction." Then there's "Midget Porn Star." (He jokingly offered that one for sale in a plain brown paper bag.) Danny also made location-specific shirts for the annual conventions. For the Utah gathering he created "Utah, me short" (you have to read it aloud to get it) and "One wife, seven dwarfs: we had the idea first."

Then there was the (in)famous "Midget Petting Zoo." I assumed the phrase made reference to the obnoxious habit some people have of "petting" the heads of strangers with dwarfism, supposedly for good luck. Danny explained to me that was the main impetus for the shirt, but that it also turned out to be read as an insider reference to the meat-market atmosphere that sometimes breaks out at LPA conventions—"petting" in the sexual sense. In any case, it caused a good bit of agitation. But the T-shirt of Danny's that finally set off a firestorm within LPA showed up at the 2003 Boston convention and featured the words "Amish Midget Militia," along with a cartoon of an Amish man with dwarfism holding a musket. I took it as absurdist, an avant-garde commentary on identity politics and political correctness. And I still suppose it was. But several leaders in LPA—people who had been smarting for years about Danny's liberal use of the word "midget"—said they found it phenomenally offensive. When Danny pointed out that the ironic use of the word "midget" didn't offend all little people in the way they claimed, the objectors found a formerly Amish member of LPA and got her to say the shirt was oppressing her.

Ultimately that T-shirt—well, that plus the fact that Danny was giving kids at the convention soda straws and navy beans to create some mayhem—got him kicked out of the Boston convention and out of the organization, too. At the Boston event, Matt Roloff, the

then-president of LPA, marched up to the Shortdwarf.com booth
and handed Danny a legalized "get out" letter. This was soon followed with an official notice that his membership in LPA had been
revoked along with his convention-selling privileges. (Incidentally,
this is the same Matt Roloff who now makes a small fortune via the
TLC "reality" show, "Little People, Big World." In an early episode,
Roloff's son can be seen wearing a Shortdwarf.com shirt.) Danny
made a deal with the cops called to escort him out of the convention
hotel: he'd give them "Amish Midget Militia" shirts if they'd lead him
out with the police car lights in full swing. The cops obliged. This, of
course, only irritated Roloff and company more.

When I called to get her thoughts on the matter, Angela Van Etten,
a very well-respected, well-liked lawyer and activist and the former
president of LPA, explained to me the political valence of the term
"midget," saying that many people within the dwarf community consider the word "midget" akin to "nigger." It's a term of derision or
mockery at worst, a term of ignorance at best. But it wasn't always
this way. In fact, when Billy Barty helped organize what became LPA
in Reno in 1957, it was under the banner "Midgets of America." At
the time, "midget" was what you wanted to be if you were a dwarf.
"Midget" meant that your limbs were proportionate to your trunk—
that your body looked like an average-sized person's, but in minia-
ture. "Dwarf" meant you had the shortened arms, legs, and fingers
typical of, say, achondroplasia—the kind of dwarfism Danny happens to have been born with. In the 1950s, an achondroplastic dwarf
like Danny would not have been anatomically privileged enough to
call himself a midget.

But somewhere along the way "midget" turned into a slur. Presumably this happened around the time when the politically conscious
people in what became LPA realized they had to take control of the
language to take control of their identities and lives. They couldn't
control "midget" or "dwarf"—those words were already out there,

already full of negative connotations—and in any case, the distinction between those two terms just caused confusion and hierarchy among people with short stature. So they re-created themselves, one and all, as "little people." Unity above diagnosis.

I learned from Van Etten that the folks who are LPA's counterparts in the UK hate the term "little people." British dwarfism advocates prefer "people of restricted growth." I can't stand "little people" either—it's the name my five year old uses to refer to his Fisher-Price toys, and I'm still laughing about the time recently when Danny was over and my son, showing Danny a toy, asked Danny, "Do you know about little people?" Danny answered, chuckling, "Oh, boy, do I know about little people!" On the other hand "people of restricted growth" sounds strangely horticultural to me, like they're victims of the Bonsai craze or something. Van Etten says that occasionally someone suggests it is time to change the name of LPA but that so far the proposals haven't gone anywhere.

After Danny got booted from LPA, I held a dinner/discussion at my house to brainstorm about what Danny should do next. The invitees included local folks that Danny had come to know and trust, plus a graduate student who was writing her thesis on grassroots political attempts to retake words like "midget," "nigger," and "queer." Over a grilled pork tenderloin and several bottles of wine, we pressed Danny on why he was so intent on using the word "midget"—what it meant to him, what he thought it could do. I noticed that, in his responses, Danny wasn't completely articulate about his own work—he couldn't always say why he did what he did—and it was then that I started to realize Danny is at some core level an artist, one who picks up on the political and personal vibrations around him and channels them into short phrases and images and performances. How else could you explain "Amish Midget Militia"?

One thing was clear, though: Danny had found, again and again, that when he was out in public in a T-shirt that had the word "midget" on it, something interesting happened. Usually the word "midget" (and all its attendant images and meanings) followed him around like an unwanted aura, creating a sort of distance between him and each stranger he would encounter. But when he put the word "midget" on his chest, it was as if he had released the pressure that existed behind the "m"-word's silent presence. The graduate student at our dinner told him this is called "resignification." By wearing the name "midget" front and center, Danny forced the first response to be to that—to the word "midget"—so that the word and its thick ideas could be exorcised.

Danny told me, for example, that he would on occasion wear one of his "midget"-themed shirts to a fraternity party where he was hired to work, and a frat boy would come up to him and say, "Wait a minute. Now I'm confused. What do you people like to be called?"

And Danny would answer, "Um, white. How about you?"

And after the awkward laugh, Danny would take a moment to talk a little about the politics of various words, and in simply being there talking, he would convince the frat boy that Danny is pretty much like everyone else—pretty much like the frat boy. Only funnier.

WHEN LEN SAWISCH helped start the Dwarf Athletic Association of America (DAAA) in 1985, he purposely used the word "dwarf" at a time when it was largely unpopular at LPA. Len told me over lunch a month or so ago that, in 1985, he knew from working through LPA that there were plenty of parents—especially sports-fanatic dads—who couldn't deal with the word "dwarf" because they couldn't deal with the fact that their kids—especially their sons—were dwarfs. But these dads wanted their dwarf sons (as they wanted all their sons) to be athletic—to power-lift, to play basketball, to be jocks. By using the word "Dwarf" in the name of the DAAA, Len made sure that these fathers would have to come to terms with the word, and in so doing would have to come to terms with their kids being dwarfs.

Len was one of the people who attended what came to be known as the Amish Midget Militia Dinner at my house. When I e-mailed Len to ask him if he'd give me an interview for this article, I was reminded that he likes to say he retired as a dwarf a few years back. But I asked him to do it as a favor to Danny and me nonetheless. Nowadays Len, who holds a PhD in psychology, works for the state of Michigan as a communications and customer technology consultant. He used to do professional disability activism as well as stand-up comedy that centered on his dwarfism—Len was featured in the 1982 Emmy-nominated documentary *Little People* and in the twenty-year follow-up, *Big Enough*—but these days he doesn't do many gigs qua dwarf. It got old for him.

Len and Danny met by accident. At the time—this was years before Danny got into the specialty product and entertainment businesses—Danny was selling Kirby vacuum cleaners door-to-door. One of the other Kirby salespeople happened to ring Len's door and encountered his wife, Lenette (yes, that's really her name), who is slightly shorter than her mate. The salesperson decided he had to send Danny back to this house, and when Lenette met Danny, she asked him to come by when Len was home. A friendship and mentorship was born. Which is not—Len hastens to add—to say that Len ever bought a vacuum cleaner from Danny.

Len occasionally expresses some level of amusement around Danny's political misadventures and some confusion about what certain Shortdwarf shirts mean, but he is invariably affectionate and supportive. I sometimes wonder if Danny actually got his impatience with political correctness from Len. I do know Len gave Danny the idea for an early T-shirt that on the front said "Real live dwarf!" and on the back "Not really. It's just a costume." When I asked Len about his reading of Danny's struggles with LPA, Len pointed to two seemingly contradictory messages that seem to circulate among the LPA membership, of whom about nine percent do some work in entertainment: first, that being a dwarf entertainer is an okay way to make a living, and second, that, if you go into dwarf entertainment, it's going to make it harder on those of us with "real" professions to make a living.

Everyone I interviewed for this article, including Len Sawisch and Angela Van Etten, was quick to point out that they personally know that working in the entertainment field means having a real profession. It is work that takes skill, talent, and determination, and only if you're good can you make a living at it. And Danny is good at it. So he knows the breadth of his market. He knows that some people are going to be attracted by the fact that one of his phone numbers is 1-866-U-Midget. But I told him not long after we met that I would personally never use the term "midget." I told him I was beginning to understand how he was using it—as Len articulates—to do a particular kind of American street theatre wrapped up in an avant-garde sort of disability activism, but that I couldn't say the "m" word. Danny looked at me with a big grin and responded, "It's just a word, Alice." I blushed and reminded him that I am a card-carrying member of humanist academia. I assured him we're never, ever allowed to say "it's just a word."

So, THIS IS the chief objection people have to the kind of work Danny does when he's working as an elf or leprechaun or arranging for other talent to appear as Mini-Me or an Oompa-Loompa: It drags down the progressive image of people with dwarfism. It objectifies them. It reiterates classic stereotypes about dwarfism and feeds a culture of oppression that many advocates have worked long and hard to overcome. In this sense, it is like a minstrel show at best, prostitution at worst.

Danny's basic response to this is libertarian. He feels he should be allowed to do whatever he wants with his body—even dwarf-tossing, a bizarre act in which a short-statured person is thrown about by taller people, if he is stupid enough or desperate enough to take on the physical risk and social grief. (Incidentally, he's not.) But when I talked to Angela Van Etten, she clearly had a different take. She argued that these things must be understood as issues of common decency—that, just as we don't allow prostitution because it is dangerous, dehumanizing, and affronts common decency, we shouldn't allow something as risky and degrading as dwarf-tossing. While she did not explicitly object to leprechaun- or Mini-Me-type acts, she did evince her highest regard for performers like Peter Dinklage (star of *The Station Agent* and now *Death at a Funeral*) who have become mainstream actors in serious roles. And she had little patience for the kind of comical, stature-specific gig Steve Vento does, where he walks around a Milwaukee Mexican restaurant that he co-owns wearing a large sombrero, the brim covered in chips with a bowl of dip nestled in the top of the hat. (Restaurant patrons are encouraged to partake in the snacks, which they can easily reach, given Vento's height.) "It certainly makes you cringe," she said. "I wouldn't go there. It's like, well, that's a shame. But the organization [LPA] didn't do anything to try to stop it."

If it were up to Anthony Soares, LPA's former vice president for public relations, the organization might try. Soares was one of the people most angered by Danny's T-shirts, and as Adelson's book notes, Soares has publicly denounced Steve Vento's sombrero routine as barbaric, humiliating, degrading, and disgusting. Soares is also well known for attacking former Secretary of Labor Robert Reich for making jokes about his own short stature on the campaign trail.

All of which is kind of strange, given that Soares himself campaigned for public office under the slogan "a councilman who will stand up for the little guy" and given that his publicity shots were explicitly taken from the vantage of a tall person looking down at him.

Pressed about using public interest in his dwarfism for political gain, Soares' response was simply this: "It's been a disadvantage enough times that I might as well use it to my advantage." Hmmm . . . the same line Danny had long used to justify his own work.

I asked Danny recently how he felt about this—about folks like Matt Roloff and Tony Soares giving him such grief and then turning around and using public interest in their bodies to their personal advantage. And, by the way, how did he feel about some folks on the online dwarfism lists giving Roloff and Soares grief for their occasionally stereotypical public performances? Danny answered that people should just cut Roloff and Soares some slack. It's not easy being out there in the public eye, and it's their lives, their bodies, their self-representations. And, he added with a wink, maybe the more Roloff and Soares do this, the more they'll understand what Danny does.

BY HIS OWN admission, Paul Steven Miller is the ultimate assimilated dwarf. Now a distinguished legal scholar on faculty at the University of Washington in Seattle, Paul was appointed by President Clinton in 1994 to be an Equal Employment Opportunity Commissioner. When we met at an ethics workshop on pediatric limb-lengthening surgeries a couple of years ago, Paul was finishing out his second term with the EEOC. (He introduced himself by saying, "I'm a civil rights attorney in the Bush administration. I have a lot of free time.")

In a phone interview, I put to Paul the argument that when Danny does an act that makes reference to his dwarfism and the stereotypes associated with it, he's making everyone with dwarfism look bad.

"That sort of gets tiring," Paul responded, "and he didn't sign up for that." He went on:

> Not everyone in LPA can or should be Paul Miller, Lee Kitchens, Ruth Ricker [a national disability activist], Matt Roloff, or

whatever. There's a wider range. And he's not hurting or dam-aging anyone—he's being a little bit more in your face. That may ultimately be offensive to average-size parents of children with dwarfism in LPA who think we have to be hyper-normal, but look, I understand my own life, and it's pretty hyper-normal. I worked hard, excelled, went to Ivy League schools, worked for the President. . . . I couldn't do what Danny did, but I think that's OK.

Paul expressed frustration at the idea that everyone should try to grow up to Be Like Paul. "I think that there is room outside of a monolithic Father Knows Best kind of image of who dwarfs are in America."

Paul likened the reaction to Danny's work—especially to his use of the word "midget"—to reactions to the work of black male comedians like Richard Pryor, Chris Rock, and Dave Chappelle, who have channeled and spoken the reality of race, racial identity, and racism as they have seen it. "He's holding up a mirror to the LPA community and especially to society and calling it like he sees it. . . . [He's] saying out loud what he imagines a lot of people are thinking. I sort of get that. I can appreciate that." I asked Paul why his own attitude seems to differ in that way from a lot of other public figures who are little people. Paul speculated, "in some way I am secure enough, or confident enough, or egocentric enough that [what Danny's doing] doesn't intimidate me or freak me out, or offend me in any way. Because what he's doing in a sense doesn't distract from who I am."

Of course Paul can literally afford to laugh at himself—to wear the "Midget Porn Star" shirt he bought from Danny a few years back—given that he's also got a resume that's as long as a government white paper and a dozen pictures of himself working alongside the presi-dent. But I felt nonetheless like he had hit on something with his likening of Danny to black comedians like Pryor. Because, even though Danny's critics feel like he's just metaphorically stepping up in blackface, shucking-and-jiving, he always seems to be doing something more. Messing with his audience's minds while making them laugh. Taking the stare and answering it confidently with a joke, first at his expense, and then at theirs.

Danny is no dupe; he knows how to manage image and representation like any professional actor. Paul is right in suggesting that Danny knows what Pryor knew—that performance that can at first seem exploitative can actually be subversive, even progressive. The Emory University disability studies scholar Rosmarie Garland-Thomson has written about this, noting how self-display "provides a medium for positive identity politics and an opportunity to protest cultural images of disabled people." Although Danny's clients don't typically hire him to come and do explicit disability activism, I've noticed he almost always manages to naturally do at least a little. This is because, as Garland-Thomson argues, the performer uses the opportunity of the performance to control how she or he is seen, to alter how people with that body type are understood, to change the terms of the discussion. Look at Danny as he's working the room, and you can see he's necessarily reworking how the room is thinking about the short guy.

Danny does this by being out. As out as out gets: "Go ahead, call me a midget. I can use another felony conviction." Or this: This culture thinks dwarfs are elves? OK, it's Christmas, so today I'm working as an elf, but I'm not going to just stand there for you to look at—I'm going to talk to you and make you treat me like a human. You're going to get that this is an act.

Maybe this is part of what bugs a certain set of people in LPA—that Danny is so out, when they're just tired of the problem of always being out when you just want to get by. It's a classic problem I've seen in groups like LPA that try to do both support and advocacy:

the people who want support pretty much want it because they're not ready to be too out. Meanwhile, the people who do the advocacy and the public work are by definition out, done with shame, tired of shame—and all attempts to squelch their being out feels like a reinstatement of the shame the group was originally formed to dispel. Arguments ensue about whether privacy is the same as shame. People make claims about who really has the right or obligation to represent the identity group. And on and on.

Danny's critics want to claim that what he does must be a manifestation of internalized self-hatred. But it looks to me like maybe it's just the opposite—self-acceptance, self-confidence, a serious sense of empowerment. In this sense, Danny is indeed living in the tradition of the freak show. James Taylor, who has studied and written about the history of anatomical exhibitions, reminded me of this when I called to ask him about how he reads Danny's work. People think the "freaks" of old-time sideshows were essentially held captive and forced on display for the pleasure of a gawking public. But in fact most people who exhibited their anatomical curiosities made a point of remaining in control of the show—deciding how they would be seen while maximizing profit and maximizing the sense of being unique, valuable, powerful.

The customer would basically pay to go and meet the featured star. And what would happen? The star would do some kind of little act, and then just talk to the customer. "What little else went on with that person's act," Taylor notes, "usually paled by comparison with the audience's chance to feel up close and friendly with someone who was different." (Danny tells me this is so true. Audience members want a picture with him, want his autograph, just to feel like they got a little extra connection.) If the customer acted like a jerk, the star made a point of making the customer look even more like a jerk. This was all standard practice—the pay up front, the act, the personal connection, the control. In the nineteenth century, Chang and Eng Bunker, who coined the name "the Siamese Twins" to advertise themselves, used exactly this formula to make a fortune. Same with Charles Stratton, the guy who billed himself as General Tom Thumb.

"It's not demeaning to the people doing it," Taylor insists. He adds, "Danny is one of my heroes in the business. . . . If you can get into the business nowadays and have his attitude about who you are, what you are, and go into it with the knowledge of how people see you, and you can work that with a sense of humor and enough finesse to poke fun at yourself, but also take it seriously enough to make your living off of it, that's success in this business."

What about the claim that an act like Danny's just reinstates the image of the person with dwarfism as a freak? When I put this to Taylor, he immediately recalled a maxim told to him by Johnny Meah, a man Taylor describes as one of the greatest sideshow banner-painters who ever lived: You only ever meet a freak once. After that, it's just a guy. It's inevitable. You think you're coming to see something totally different, then it turns out it's just a person in a different shape. "Once you meet these people, you don't feel compelled to stare at them again; they're what they are—they're who they are." Taylor's point reminded me of the way that, when interviewed by the *New York Daily News* about the Fidelity bachelor party, Thomas Bruderman's father assured the press, "There was only one dwarf. His name was Dan. He wasn't a clown or anything. He was just a nice short person."

I've asked Danny about that—whether he ever considers that he might drive himself out of business by humanizing people with dwarfism during his acts. Once people understand he's "just a guy," maybe they won't want to hire him anymore. But he says he isn't worried. Most of his customers are repeat clients. They hire him the first time out of curiosity. They hire him the second and third and fourth time because he's funny, personable, and professional.

———

I WAS SECRETLY starting to find the idea of the sombrero act really funny. Particularly after I talked with James Taylor, I found that, anytime I pulled up the mental image of a short guy serving chips and dip out of a big hat, I couldn't stop chuckling. Was I losing my moral center? Was I becoming an exploitative jerk? Or was I maybe finally getting comfortable with the idea that some people are really short, and that human variety is kind of a cosmic joke?

In early February last year, I met Danny for coffee at a cafe near my house. Between fielding business calls, he told me about an inquiry the office staff had triaged to him the day before, a classic Valentine's Day call from a new customer. It went pretty much like this:

Novice: "Is this . . . um . . . is this the number I call for . . . um. . . . What do I call you people?"

Danny: "Most people call me Danny."

Novice: "I was thinking about hiring someone—a dwarf—to deliver a Valentine's Day greeting to my girlfriend. Is that weird?"

Danny: "I dunno. Do you love her?"

Novice: "Yes."

Danny: "Well, then it's not as weird as if you didn't love her."

Novice: "But, I mean, why would I hire a dwarf to do this?"

Danny: "Maybe you love her, and maybe you've told her you love her in a hundred other ways, and maybe you want to do something different, to get her attention? So you want to have a dwarf do it."

Novice: "Yeah, I guess so. Are you a dwarf?"

Danny: "Yes. Are you?"

Novice: "No."

Danny: "Well, then, I guess you need me. Shall we talk rates?"

I myself talked rates with Danny not long after that. In early March, just before my fortieth birthday—realizing the cosmic joke aging surely is—I asked Danny if he would do me a favor and work my party for an hour. He was going to be there anyway as a guest, but I wanted to know if he'd let me pay him for one hour of his professional time. I wanted him to do the sombrero thing, and I wanted him, while he was serving the chips and dip, to pose one question over and over again to my academic friends:

"Resignification, or dehumanization?"

I had only ever hired Danny once before. Years ago, when I was working on the twins book, I had contracted with him to go to the Mütter Museum at the College of Physicians in Philadelphia and tell me what he thought of the displays of dwarfs' remains there. Some of them are pickled, some dried. One particular case at the Mütter features the skeleton of Mary Ashberry, a nineteenth-century woman with achondroplasia dwarfism who apparently survived via sexual prostitution, and who died in childbirth. The Mütter has her skeleton posed holding the skull of her fetus. Danny came home with this reaction to the display: "You want dehumanization? That's dehumanization!" He was as upset as I'd ever seen him.

So Danny came and worked my party for an hour, and stayed as a guest for another two or three. Most of my friends knew him from my previous parties where they were guests together, so they weren't really playing along when he asked them the question I had paid him to ask. Like typical academics, they wanted mostly to talk about what they had written about dehumanization or resignification or other vague postmodern concepts. I was afraid Danny was going to charge me extra for having to listen to all this. But he was a good sport.

And the truth is, although we celebrated my birthday that year on March 18, my birthday actually falls on March 17: St. Patrick's Day. I never celebrate it on that day, partly because I don't especially like the color green or large crowds of drunks, and partly because I'm still smarting from believing my parents who told me when I was little that the big parade in New York every year was in my honor. ("I don't get it," I finally said to them. "We're Polish. Why a big Irish parade?") But that year, because I was working on this article, I decided to recognize St. Patrick's Day just long enough to stop down at the local brewpub and watch Danny work his annual gig. As a consequence, this is what I'm going to remember from my fortieth, more than the sombrero:

A dwarf walks into a bar. He's dressed as a leprechaun. He starts working the crowd. It's physically exhausting work—he spends a lot of time standing and bending his head back, so he can talk to the other folks standing taller than him—but he seems to be enjoying himself nevertheless. The scene is mostly college students wearing Kelly green, drinking green beer, taking pictures on their cell phones. The bar's owners are paying the dwarf well, but it's clear they're making a tidy profit on both the beer and the entertainment.

Folks come up to talk to the leprechaun, because it is, after all, St. Patrick's Day. They soon learn his name is Danny, they tell them their first names, and they joke around pleasantly with him. Occasionally someone makes an ass of himself in response to Danny's act, and when that happens, Danny takes a few extra performative steps to make sure it's clear who the ass really is. The vast majority of the encounters are polite, upbeat, in a holiday spirit. The conversations often end in a firm handshake and a genuine smile. A few people recognize him from previous encounters, and those people come over to say a warm hello.

Danny comes off looking ever better from these small encounters. The longer he's there, the longer I watch him, the more obvious it is he's a winner. And the more it's clear the people around him get that. Yeah, he's a dwarf, a midget, a little person, a person of restricted growth, whatever. Yeah, he carries around all the medical and social challenges of his achondroplasia. But mostly he's a nice guy with a great sense of humor and a sore back from standing up working so long. He's just a guy. And I'm thinking, Johnny Meah was dead-on. You only ever meet a freak once.

Chicago Transit Priority

WOOD-TANG.COM

I've been a little lazy about getting around town since I bought a hybrid car. When faced with a decision whether to drive or take public transit, too often I opt for the former out of sheer selfishness, rationalizing that since I'm using roughly half the fuel as everyone else, I'm allowed to drive twice as much. But now that gas costs north of $4.00 a gallon, promising only to go higher, that choice is no longer about a squishy, moral obligation to reduce consumption and preserve the planet. It's starting to get expensive. And since I live in Chicago, a city with an extensive public transit system, I've decided to ride the train or the bus whenever possible. I might have been shamed into it because I finally got around to watching *An Inconvenient Truth,* but I figure that since I already went crazy replacing all the lightbulbs in my house with compact fluorescents, it's the next best thing I can do.

One of my excuses for driving, aside from the electric sound of sanctimony purring from beneath my car's hood, has always been that I'm usually schlepping around my son Carter. "You can't expect me to haul a stroller onto that crowded bus, can you?" I planned to say to Al Gore if he accosted me at my regular Shell station one day. "I need a car seat. And room for a diaper bag. And drink holders for his sippy cups. And air-conditioning. And an iPod jack plus Bluetooth so I can listen to my podcasts and take phone calls hands-free." Al would slink away at this point, I imagined, muttering, "He's right, he's right" in his Tennessee drawl, despondent and ashamed for asking me to sacrifice my baby's comfort to save the planet.

Now that Carter is big enough to walk and pay for his own fare, though, he loves public transit. Love isn't a strong enough word, actually. When Carter sees the Blue Line train rumbling into our stop, he hops up and down, hooting and clapping his hands like a chimpanzee. It's Thomas the Tank Engine come to life. "Calm down, calm down," I say, hoisting him over the six-inch gap between the platform and the train car. "Now go pick a seat that doesn't smell like pee."

We've ridden the train to Grandma's house on the north side. We've ridden it downtown to buy the good coffee from Intelligentsia. We rode it to a book festival to have his picture taken with Curious George. Mostly, though, we ride the train home from school. Carter's preschool is about two and a half miles from our house. It's no more than a fifteen-minute drive, even with traffic, basically straight north on a major street. My wife drops him off on her way to work, and I pick him up after lunch. Taking the bus there takes at least thirty minutes, depending on how long I have to wait for one to show up, and the train can take up to forty-five minutes, including a transfer.

It's all a hassle, frankly, and all talk of environmental and budgetary concern is just altruistic bullshit. I doubt even Al Gore would disapprove of a fifteen-minute drive in a hybrid. But it's bigger than saving a few bucks on gas. Every Monday, Wednesday, and Friday, I trudge down to the nearest stop, a half hour before I'd need to leave if I were driving my nice, efficient car, because riding the train home from school is the biggest event of my son's day. I don't have the heart to deny him that joy, or myself the privilege of witnessing it.

WHEN YOU RIDE the train with a kid, at least one that talks as much as mine does, people seem to feel comfortable talking to you. One of the first times we rode the train, we sat down across the aisle from a middle-aged man who was built like a fireplug, muscular and stocky. He was dressed in slacks with a tight, silky black T-shirt that showed off his biceps, the way you'd dress for work if you were built like that.

He was wearing a wired cell-phone earpiece, and kept trying to talk on the phone while we roared through a subway tunnel. He cupped the microphone up to his mouth and put his finger in his other ear, while I silently mocked him. He caught my eye a couple times and I kept looking away, afraid he was going to call me out for staring at him. Then he pointed to Carter and said, "Excuse me. Does he spend a lot of time with his daddy?"

"I'm his dad," I said, wondering who else he thought I might be. A brother? An uncle? A male-nanny (manny)?

"Oh, you're his daddy? Wow," he said. "That's so good to see a boy spending time with his father. We have a whole generation of boys being raised by women."

I glossed over my situation for him, saying I worked from home and picked him up from school, leaving out the part about how my "work" nets roughly enough per year to buy a nice couch. When he got off a few stops later, he smiled, shook my hand, and said, "God bless you, man."

I sat there and felt downright saintly. Not only was I saving the environment and our family's finances by riding the train, I was saving my son from being coddled by a bunch of women. Instead, he'll grow up to be manly, independent, and strong enough to find a woman to coddle him later in life like I did.

CARTER AND I have been commuting home from school this way long enough now that he has a routine. I carry him on my shoulders to the station, he scoots under the turnstile while I pay, and hops down the stairs to the platform. When we get on the train, we circle like a dog deciding where to sleep before we pick a suitable seat, then he sits up on his knees to look out the window.

One time we sat across from a woman with her legs stretched across two seats, looking quite comfortable. "He loves to ride the train, does he?" she asked, indicating Carter.

"It's his favorite," I said.

"Really? Ooh, I'm scared of the train," she said, stretching out a little more in her makeshift business class cabin. She was wearing a white tank top pulled up to reveal a potbelly, and had the name "Nene" tattooed down her left bicep in blocky navy blue letters. She continued to ask the standard questions about Carter's age, if he goes to school, etc., while he clung to my arm and shielded his eyes. I wished I could do the same.

Nene was quiet for a few minutes, then got up and shoved a pair of half-unwrapped Dum-Dum suckers into his face and said, "Here baby, you want a sucker?" Carter finally lit up and reached out his hand, but I intercepted them and told her, "We'll save these for his dessert after lunch." This pleased Nene, and she left us alone the rest of the ride, stopping to say goodbye as she rubbed her belly and got off at her stop.

When Carter and I finally got off, I immediately threw away the suckers and launched into the "Don't take candy from strangers" lecture. He seemed to buy into it, except for the part about why I had just taken candy from a stranger myself.

"You know that lady, that's why you took the suckers?" he asked.

"No, but I was just trying to be nice to her. It was easier than saying no," I said.

"But if you give me the suckers, it's okay now?"

"No, because they came from that lady first, and we don't know her."

He was quiet as we walked the rest of the way up the ramp to street level. Once we were outside the station, he asked, "Can I have some candy when we get home?"

"Sure," I said, and lifted him onto my shoulders for the walk home.

Grasshopper

MARGARET CONWAY

"I write nonfiction because I have no other choice," says Margaret Conway. *"The characters who clamor inside my head refuse to be fictionalized or tethered to a conventional plot. . . . I value the supple, capacious medium of creative nonfiction, where there's ample room to wrestle with a character's baffling complexities before letting her take over, as she's determined to do. Also, writing needs its wild side, its far frontier. Which is why I pray that the medium does not allow itself to become codified, regulated, explained. Let the mustangs run free. Let there be one last place on a writer's earth that keeps to its essential mystery."* "Grasshopper," an outcast chapter from an unpublished memoir, appeared *in* Cimarron Review.

The year I turned twelve my father purchased his first car. As with nearly every major move in our life, it was my great-uncle who acted as facilitator. He taught my father to drive, steering him away from heavy traffic onto narrow lanes that meandered past dairy farms and fields thick with tall green tessellated corn. On the empty roads around Douglassville and Birdsboro, the two men would have had ample leisure to check out the scenery and re-play the latest race they'd been to at Monmouth, Uncle John scanning the racing paper spread across his narrow lap. John would have remained on the side-lines during the driving test while my father maneuvered the dented station wagon with the ancient pails in back and the big paperhanging brushes clogged with paste that gave off a smell so cloying that I once had to vomit out the car window.

Though a fair-weather Catholic, my father likely prayed that during the test neither the back flap nor the back doors of Uncle's wagon would fly open, as sometimes happened, giving the car the look of a large flightless bird struggling to become airborne. After the miraculously successful test, and giddy with victory, they hit the used-car lot. With no particular make or model in mind, they simply intended to get the most they could for the cash in my father's wallet.

Since I am unsure of the origin of those four hundred bucks, I can only surmise that out of my father's wages he put aside a five or a ten each week until he'd amassed the necessary sum. But squirreling away fives and tens, keeping track of a thickening bundle of bills in his sock drawer, would have been out of character. My father's character fault lay in the fact that, although dutiful and hardworking, he seemed to care not at all for money or solid possessions. A bank balance was, to him, the ultimate abstraction: invisible money. He never minded handing over his pay packet to my mother because once he had "rendered unto Caesar," as he put it, he could freely, and without guilt, do what he loved to do—read, visit the track, lose himself in the neon-lit womb of a neighborhood bar.

Money passed through his hands and into the widening sea of the family's needs. He functioned merely as a conduit. His seven kids always required something. Not much left by the end of the week. So it's likely that John lent him the four hundred, to be repaid at some time in the hazy, indeterminate future.

One thing I do recall on that summer-into-autumn day is my mother, back at the house, grousing about how Uncle didn't know crap about cars. "Driving for all these years, and still doesn't know what's under the hood. And *this* is the man who's going to advise your father?"

Even at twelve, I knew what my father would do. I envisioned him in the lemony light of the wide-open car lot up on Ridge Pike, putting a question to the salesman about "miles per gallon" or "horsepower"—the question being pedantic, since he scarcely could have cared less about horsepower or anything else to do with an automobile's innards or performance. The negotiations were a face-saving device, so he could tell my mother that he'd acquitted himself respectably in the high-stakes exchange of buying a car. Truth is, he would have itched to part with the four hundred. Then off to the bar, he and Uncle, for a couple of cool ones.

THE 1950S WAS the decade of the family sedan. To own a car became an American birthright. Without an auto you were somehow inauthentic, and I saw us that day as having moved into a whole new category: the independent and self-propelled, the drivers as opposed to the driven. No more waiting for Uncle to take us food shopping. No more being crammed, all nine of us, in the back of Uncle's flap-doodle of a station wagon. No more stinky paste pails. But that was me. My father didn't buy a car simply to fit in. He needed one for work.

By the time we got a car, my father had been working at the B.F. Goodrich plant in Oaks, Pennsylvania, for eight years. He was to put in fourteen additional years at the tire factory, but had he known that at the time, he'd probably have committed suicide like the man who'd given him rides to work each night. They'd gravitated to each other because they both loved books, good music, foreign languages. They were what has been termed, somewhat patronizingly, I think, working-class intellectuals. Because no man is an island, I know my father grieved for his dead friend, but meanwhile his transport had dried up, and he couldn't very well walk the five miles to Oaks. Not at that hour.

He worked the midnight-to-eight shift, so that his "day" was the reverse of ours. He'd wake a little before eleven, spoon instant coffee into a cup, then don his workclothes while the water rolled to a boil. By 11:20 he was hiking the quarter mile to Main Street, where he caught an Oaks-bound bus. At that hour, buses could be unreliable. Arriving even five minutes late for your shift pissed off the foreman, and a hostile foreman could render your work night considerably less pleasant.

Besides, eight other people depended on the paycheck.

"I think," said Uncle dryly, "you'll be requiring a car."

I HOPE I can be forgiven for the letdown I felt on seeing what pulled up in front of our house that September afternoon. I had pictured something streamlined and loaded with chrome. A cool car: two-toned, in the style of the day, or a dazzling shade of royal blue or fire-engine red. Instead, our new auto, the same dull green as my father's workpants, appeared stunted and misshapen, far too small for a family the size of ours.

But we had a car, I told myself. An actual car! Now we needed no longer feel inferior to neighbors up and down the street, as they backed ostentatiously out of their deep-black driveways.

My mother and we kids crowded the front walk as my father, triumphantly returned from Bob Gale's Used Autos, strode toward us, long-legged Uncle loping close behind, his strands of white hair blown to the far side of his pink skull, and his sand-colored cardigan buttoned unevenly. Both men wore the sappy, red-faced look that meant they'd made a stopover on the way home. What surprised me was the way my mother, normally eaten up by resentment over the second-rate goods that furnished our lives, seemed not at all to mind the distinctly unbeautiful car—a turgid, crouching thing that resembled a gigantic grasshopper.

Worse still, she, in short shorts and a chartreuse halter top, her five small sons clustered about her bare legs on the browning lawn, became positively kittenish with my father—a sickening display, considering the way they were normally at each other's throats.

John, the bachelor uncle, catching the intimate tone between my parents, began backing away in embarrassment. "Hem," he said. "Guess I should be getting along." No one paid him the least attention.

Instead, we listened raptly to details of the purchase.

"I test-drove it, you bet I did," my father was crowing. "Gunned the motor, and boy did she go. Children, don't ever be fooled by appearances. That car can outpace any young punk doing chicken-runs down Ridge Pike."

Her hand coyly over her mouth, my mother giggled.

Pathetic, I thought. Byron Wilde or any of the guys who hung out at the steak shop could have run him right off the road. Traitorous, though, to entertain such a thought on my father's big day, so I piped up and politely asked what make of car it was.

"Why, it's a Studebaker. Not exactly built for beauty, but you'll never find a more serviceable auto."

"Can we go for a ride?" my mother pleaded.

"I take it you mean now," my father teased.

"George, the kids have been waiting all day."

Right then it hit me that while we were off at school or with friends, or my father was at work, the bar, the track, my mother had been trapped in the house with a bunch of kids. She and my father never went anywhere. What did she care if our car looked like a grass-hopper? Hell, it had four wheels and it could go.

"Margaret," said my father in a dangerously controlled tone of voice. (This man, so detached about material possessions, was not so about insubordination on the part of his kids. The belt was coming off with increasing frequency.) "Do I detect any reservations about our new automobile?"

My mother shot me a warning look that said, *Don't go spoiling our fun.*

"Nice car," I said. "Honest. I like it."

My father's face collapsed into a smile. He patted the Studebaker's flank, saying, "Now that Margaret has given her seal of approval, what do you say we take it for a spin?"

A great cheer went up from the others. In their high-top Keds, they jumped up and down around my mother.

Daintily, as if fussing with the flounces of an evening dress, she settled herself in the passenger seat, one of the boys between her and my father and another on her lap. The others squeezed into the back. I remained standing on the grass. No way was I about to crowd into the belly of that grasshopper with all those little kids: their sticky hands, their milk-breath, their sweaty bare legs. I looked at them, crammed in the semi-gloom of the backseat behind a sort of port-hole window, and tried to hide the contempt I was beginning to feel for people who so easily, so cringingly, surrendered their dignity in return for a quick thrill. At twelve, I expected a little more from life.

There'd be time enough to ride in the new car. Though he himself no longer attended mass, my father might roll out of bed on a Sunday morning to give my sister and me a lift to church. Goodbye to walk-ing the long road between cornfield and horse pasture, scuffing our patent-leather shoes. Eileen and I, in topper coats and veiled hats, would be chauffeured to church.

My father ducked his head to see past my mother through the diminutive window. "You'll not be joining us, Margaret Anne?"

"Not today," I mumbled. "I'm supposed to meet Ginger."

"Well, la-di-da," he said, fiddling with the shift. "Your loss." The heavily freighted car bucked and shuddered—he was not yet used to the gears—and then surged down the road toward the open countryside.

WEARING SLEEVELESS BLOUSES and cotton shorts, Ginger and I walked miles to showcase our legs. We hiked past the Pennsylvania & Western depot and the Conte Luna spaghetti factory to the food-fragrant east end of town, where the only audience we attracted was a car full of greasers who veered near enough to shout, "Hey, youse! Grow something up top and we'll come back and marry you!"

"Told you," said Ginger. "We shoulda wore falsies."

"I don't have any." And couldn't imagine the embarrassment of buying them.

Tired, dispirited, I accepted a ride home from Ginger's dad. No use walking all that way when nobody'd notice me anyway. Besides, it was well past nine. By now, our road with its rare streetlights would be densely, scarily dark.

As we puttered along with the windows up, my shoulders slumped at the prospect of the shrieking reprimand I was sure to receive from my mother. From within the smoky enclosure of Mr. Nowicki's car, I tried to devise a strategy for blocking out the sound of her voice. My dread increased as we crunched onto the gravel where road met sidewalk outside our house. Bad news: it was Saturday night. My father would be there, to add muscle to my mother's gripes against me. And even more so, considering how lovey-dovey they'd been earlier in the day.

"Looks like you got company," said Mr. Nowicki.

Blinking into the darkness beyond his windshield, I spied the hulking, unfamiliar shape. Intent on my own ambitions that day, I'd almost forgotten about the grasshopper. So . . . they'd had their ride. They had christened the new car, the other eight of them. More and more, I was distancing myself from these people and wasn't sure whether that represented a good or a bad thing.

"Nah," I replied dully. "It's ours. My father bought a car today."

"He did? Well, isn't that nice," said Nowicki.

As I crept up the walk, I hugged my bare arms. Early September, though tonight might turn cold. The damp air shivered, threatening autumn, then winter. I felt tempted to make a run for the woods across the road. Hide there till morning.

I hated the fear I felt. Hated them for making me feel this way.

Oddly, the front door had been left ajar. A wide strip of light punctuated the darkness. Perhaps they'd been worried about me. Inside the house, my mother sat huddled in a corner of the couch with the youngest, a toddler, in her lap. "Did you see it?" she demanded.

She held onto the child as if he were a teddy bear, absentmindedly stroking his fine brown hair. The other boys would be asleep by now, but Eileen sat at the dinette table examining what looked like a laceration on her elbow.

"See what? What's going on?"

My mother lifted her head, fixing me with a dead-eyed look. "Weren't you the smart one. You sure knew when to stay away."

"Where's Dad?"

"Your father crashed the car."

"He—crashed it?" The first time out? What about the four hundred dollars, and us, as proud owners of a family sedan?

"I don't feel like talking anymore tonight. Stephen chipped a tooth. I wrenched my shoulder."

My father's armchair, his reading chair, sat ominously empty.

———

THE MORNING AFTER the crash, my mother sat alone at the table, sipping Nescafé. When I came downstairs dressed for mass, she said, "Sit down. You can go later."

"There *is* no 'later.' This is the last mass."

"God'll forgive you. Sit."

She passed me a glass of milk. The clink of glass on Formica was the only sound in the house. The others must have been sleeping in.

Seemed they'd been having a grand old time, singing "Davy Crockett," all the verses, while my father kept urging them to notice the "turning leaves," the first reds and yellows of the season in the Pennsylvania countryside.

"But I was just quiet," added my mother. "Glad to be going somewhere."

After they'd driven north for twenty miles or so, they came into Souderton. That's where it happened. She remembered an underpass, then a pole. My father, struggling with the wheel, crying, "Mary! I can't turn this goddamn wheel!" The steering mechanism had locked. She let the facts tumble out, without the usual rhetorical flourishes: the embellished details, the narrative drawn into a thin, vibrating wire of suspense. She hurried past the part where they'd smashed into the pole, the part where the Souderton people ("so nice") drove our family home and even arranged, at my father's request, to have the car towed back as well.

"So the car can be fixed?"

"No, it cannot be fixed," she said indignantly. "It's totaled."

"Then—"

"Don't ask me why he had that thing brought back here." I could feel us closing in on the real story, the narrative that rumbled beneath mere accident facts. "And don't ask why he won't go up to Bob Gale, that crook, and demand our money back."

"Maybe Uncle—"

"Don't mention that man! I blame all this on him. But guess what reason your father's giving?"

"Reason for what?"

"For not getting our money back! Are you paying attention?"

"I *am*!"

"Says it's like placing a bet: you may win, you may lose. Meanwhile, the creep on Ridge Pike is laughing up his sleeve at the two live ones who bought that lemon."

Now we were getting into old grudges between her and my father, between her and my great-uncle, stuff I was not remotely interested in. I peeked through the venetian blind, to see what daylight might reveal. Someone—probably my father—had draped an old army blanket over the wreckage.

THE RAVAGED CAR remained in place for three months. Within a week the blanket had blown off. Late autumn rains drummed against the body of the Studebaker. Floppy red maple leaves drifted down, pasting themselves onto the wet roof, the crushed hood. One night a prankster, or maybe a neighbor sick of that eyesore, caved in the windshield. December snow sifted through the gouged glass, piling whitely on the passenger seat. A blizzard buried our auto under a foot of snow, rendering it identical to every other car in sight: a fat white shape in a white landscape.

The snow melted. Once again, kids at school began needling me about the junk-heap in front of our house. People walking by expressed their distaste. One woman used a term I'd never heard: "Tobacco Road."

My father, who re-read James Joyce's *Ulysses* every year of his adult life, who spoke Berlitz Italian and could sing operatic arias and quote with ease from Dickens and Shakespeare, could not manage to have that wreck removed. My mother nagged, raged, implored, but his old inertia had set in. Was this something to do with the Irish temperament—an inherited lowering of the give-a-shit factor after eight hundred years of English rule—or simply that after standing on a factory floor in front of a high-decibel machine, surrounded by other high-decibel machines, my father had developed a sort of Yogic detachment, the power that made it possible for him to read difficult books while seemingly oblivious to my brothers' tumbling and brawling all around his chair?

One morning the car was gone, vanished in the night, and my father waved away any questions about its removal.

I found that I missed the wretched thing. After all, I was the one who'd never ridden in it, never smelled its leather seats or experienced its horsepower. I was the one who could know it only posthumously. Toward the end I'd been sneaking out there to witness its disintegration, having already learned that breakdown can be far more fascinating than unobstructed growth. I thought of the log I sat on in the woods, its crumbling underside that supported an entire ecosystem: wild grasses, earthworms, ants, beetles, and wet black soil that exuded a rich, ripe smell of decay.

The impact of the crash had torqued the body of the car to the left, so that its windshield reflected the trees across the road. On windy gray December days, tree skeletons swam black and watery in the intact portion of the glass, and I'd stand for long periods, puzzling over why this sight pleased me more than our Christmas tree, or a winter sunset, or the window display at Novell's.

Ever the smart aleck of the schoolyard, I spouted big words I'd heard my father use. I won spelling bees and kept a vocabulary list. Now, though, I needed words in the aggregate: sentences, whole paragraphs to capture the mutable beauty of that dead car as it fell to the elements.

What Comes Out

DAWNELLE WILKIE

This story, which appeared in The Truth About the Fact, *focuses on the bare and unnerving reality of the inner workings of an abortion clinic. Says Dawnelle Wilkie, "To write about what I experienced and witnessed working in women's health . . . required the unflinching honesty and compassion that are necessary in creative nonfiction."*

We do not talk about What Comes Out. We hold it close like a secret that has the power to undo us. When asked, we describe it in strange unphysical terms. We obfuscate. We use soft archaic language. The Contents of the Uterus. Tissue. Menstrual Products. The Products of Conception. The last one is our favorite; it's also the accurate medical term, though we shorten it to P.O.C. in daily use.

When asked we have appropriate scripts depending on who is doing the asking. Over the phone is basic (you never know who is on the other end of the line), in person is more descriptive, in person during counseling is the most descriptive but done in the most obscure terms and with little attention to detail. The voice must be soft and slow in the last instance. In the other two instances, one can rely solely on one's professional voice.

We stick to the script. Always.

What comes out? What do we do with it? Here is the truth. This is not the script.

There is blood, though perhaps less than you would imagine. Or perhaps not. Usually two or three cups at the most. (Imagine a Pyrex measuring cup, the four-cup size, the one you use to make brownies or to measure cut strawberries.) The amount of blood is in direct relation to how far along you are. It's a menstrual period (plus some) that happens in the span of five minutes.

When the doctor is finished with you—when you are lying on the table and the surgical tech is applying pressure to your abdomen to help your cramps, or wiping your forehead because the Fentanyl has made you sweat, or giving you water because the stress has left you dry-mouthed, or standing quietly in the corner while you cry softly (or yell loudly) at your partner, your friend, your sister, your mother, your surgical tech—What Comes Out is taken to the lab. Maybe you see it leave, a bundle of blue surgical paper, and you imagine terrible things. Whatever you're imagining is probably wrong. It's mainly equipment: one speculum, one tenaculum, one ring forceps, one set of five dilators, five cotton balls, and five gauze pads. Sometimes a handheld vacuum aspirator (imagine a turkey baster), sometimes not.

In the lab, the surgical pack is unwrapped and disassembled. What Comes Out is in a small cup or a large glass jar, depending on the method of suction. Handheld suction warrants a small cup, the same kind you left your urine sample in; machine suction warrants the large glass jar. If you heard something that sounded like a small sputtering airplane or your mother's old vacuum cleaner, you had the machine. If you heard nothing but the doctor's voice and the sound of your own shaky breathing, you had the handheld. You may have also heard the keg delivery at the pool hall upstairs, though the surgical tech would have tried to muffle the thumps with Muzak and small talk.

The lab tech, another white-coated person, who may or may not have checked you in at the front desk or given you your pregnancy test results three days ago or ordered her coffee from you this morning at the drive-through, empties the contents of the cup or jar into a small colander. (Imagine rinsing spaghetti.) The purpose is to rinse away the blood. Much water is wasted this way. When the water starts to run clear through the bottom of the colander, she will take her hand and make a loose fist. It will be hard for her to make anything tighter because of the layers of gloves, both latex and PVC. She will rest her fist in the colander and start to grind slowly (imagine a mortar and pestle). Her first time doing this she was worried she would smash "something important" through the wire mesh (by this she meant a fetal part). The doctor assured her she would not. Most times it will be slippery. If you are far enough along she will feel small hard things bumping against her rings, which she now will remember she has forgotten to remove. These are bones.

Once What Comes Out has been rinsed, she will transfer it to a Pyrex baking dish (imagine casseroles) that sits on top of a small light board (imagine photography class). It contains nothing but a half inch of water and what has come out of your uterus. She will take a metal knitting needle and poke things around. Mostly what is there are little scraps of what was once your uterine lining, that sheddable disposable skin you had hoped to see a few weeks ago but didn't. What she is looking for—what she is hoping to find, what she prays will be there because if it's not you'll have to do the whole thing over again—is the pregnancy sack.

When she finds it her shoulders will relax, she will smile slightly and her eyes will soften. It is surprisingly graceful and looks like a tiny jellyfish (imagine the seashore: the gulls, the smell of seaweed, the amoebic washed-up jellyfish undulating their way back to the sea). It is transparent and at about eight or nine weeks it grows these little hair-like cilia (or is it ganglia?) that gather nutrients from the bloodstream to feed the fetus. It's thin and glows with a strange luminescence. On first viewing, one is struck dumb by its beauty and perfection. It's not large, sometimes a dime or a quarter, sometimes larger if you are further along. Sometimes the doctor can feel it coming and will stop the suction to place it on a small piece of gauze. When this happens there is much oohing and aahing by the lab tech as she floats the perfect intact sea creature of your womb in light-drenched water.

There is the fetus. Or not. Sometimes it's too small to see. Sometimes it disintegrates during suction. When it doesn't, it usually breaks into several pieces. The lab tech looks for limbs, sometimes a rib cage, sometimes a small leathery thing that will become a skull. If a foot can be found, most times attached to a leg, it is set to one side for use later. There are small organs present: a heart, lungs, a liver; intestines uncoil and float around, getting in the way of everything (imagine the seaweed wrapping around your legs that summer at the lake when you learned to swim). Other organs are too small to see. Bones (especially ones that are encased in skin, usually in the form of a hand or foot) are important and pushed to one side of the dish. The light filters through them from below, and they glow like perfect white sticks.

After all the parts have been identified and the doctor has nodded her approval, in between asking what music the lab tech is listening to and telling a story about the deer who won't stop eating her lettuces, What Comes Out must be assigned a number, a date, an age. This is done in one of two ways. If there is no fetus, the pregnancy sack is compared to a hand-drawn sketch on the wall above the counter (imagine the doctor, a failed painter who is forced to fall back on her medical degree to earn a living). The size of the sack corresponds to the number of weeks of the pregnancy; it is measured in centimeters or the more common familiar-object scale. A golf ball (imagine your boyfriend's creepy father, the way he hugs too long) would equal approximately ten weeks. Larger means more; smaller, less. Due to its size, the five-week sack is the most elusive. When one is found, the lab tech will call to other clinic workers (the ones that "do the lab" and can look and won't look away, the ones that find it all fascinating and beautiful and very seldom gross) to come and see. The five-week sack is rare and perfect—a white whale, a black pearl.

If there is a fetus the measurement is based on fetal foot length. The leg with the attached foot is held with a pair of tweezers while, in the other hand, the lab tech presses the foot against a small transparent ruler (imagine having your foot sized for new shoes). The measurement, again in centimeters, is in direct correlation to the number of weeks of the pregnancy. The lab tech, still double-gloved and sweating under layers of impermeable fabric, curses this process. She drops the leg several times in the Pyrex dish and has to tweeze it out again. Perhaps she gets hold of it at a spot where the tendon attaches to the foot and the foot flexes forward and backward and won't hold still. Perhaps the foot falls off the limb and she has to lay it, now limbless, on a gauze pad and measure it that way. When she finally gets the measurement and announces it, the doctor, too busy with her story of the deer and the lettuces, says, "Are you sure?" and the tech must measure again.

When the measurement is complete the process is done. What was once revered by the lab tech and the doctor—protected from rushing water and placed with great care in a dish, measured, sorted, cleaned, and presented—is now dumped back in the little cup and thrown in a red biohazard bucket, where it will be joined by twelve to fourteen other What Comes Outs during the day. The bucket will be collected sometime the following week by Gerry, who chain-smokes and is planning on retiring in four months.

Unless of course you have asked to see What Comes Out. If you have—though you probably haven't, almost no one does—you will see an abridged version. The lab tech will bring a small cup into the room after removing her layers of protective gear, and she will smile and say nothing. You will see the pregnancy sack floating in water. We will include some scraps of uterine lining. The doctor will explain to you what they are, and you will nod appreciatively and say "That's all?" Perhaps you suspect that we haven't shown you everything, perhaps you are smarter than we would hope you to be. If you were farther along, we will try to dissuade you from looking at fetal parts. We will explain that even most of the women who work at the clinic do not work in the lab, that they find it distasteful. We use this word: distasteful (imagine Emily Post). Most times you are pacified with looking at the ultrasound, which is grainy and indistinguishable, qualities that make us reluctant to get a new and better machine, one that would take pictures that might upset you, pictures that reveal too much.

The doctor returns to you, tells you, "Everything went just fine." You're not entirely sure what she means, but you say, "Thank you," and she leaves. You get up and get dressed and go to recovery and eat stale cookies and drink apple juice (imagine afternoon snack at preschool) and then after a while the nurse tells you you're okay and you leave. You pass the lab and see someone in a white coat reading a book and waiting for something to happen. There's music you can't quite make out. She's wearing a hairnet and has a plastic face shield pulled to the top of her head like a visor (imagine a welder's mask). She looks up at you and smiles that "I hope you're feeling okay," lame, pity smile you've seen on everyone's face since you got here.

You go home.

Perhaps this was helpful. Perhaps not. But this is the truth; this is what we avoid saying. We hide behind our scripts and clean language; we avoid words like *blood, pain, clot,* and *fear* (imagine hesitating, even now, nauseous and cold, before typing the forbidden word: *baby*). We hold this truth close and don't let it out, fearing the other side, the ones with signs, the ones with guns and websites with our names and the names of our loved ones. We cling to words like *empowerment, healing,* and the mother of all words: *choice.* We shield ourselves with euphemisms and mission statements, but this is the truth we won't even talk about among ourselves. The one we fear because there is no denying the simple truths of the body. But truth will always out, and now I have spoken its name and I am waiting for the world to crumble and our position to unravel like seaweed or intestines in a Pyrex dish. I am waiting.

(names have been changed)

STEAL YOUR IMAGINATION
(WEB.MAC.COM/IRISHDOYLE)

1.

She lay on the cushion in the library, her face pushing into the blue plastic cover, looking for cool. Her fevered body succumbed to that spot, alternating sweating and shivering. Her throat swollen. The glands angry. She ignores all the books surrounding her. The books she usually can't get enough of. This happens all the time, she whispers.

2.

The special drink they had made me tasted sweet. Sprite and chinola juice and rum. It was a breezy Saturday, the cusp of afternoon and evening, right when the mosquitoes begin emerging. We sat at a wooden table on the side of the mountain, looking down to the ocean miles away. A quick meeting. Talking business. Oh, the doctor said, and that camper you sent me a week ago, we got her tested. Pause. It came back positive.

3.

The boss stepped down into the house of white wood and concrete block. I followed behind. Concrete floor immaculately clean. Two bedrooms to the left behind the makeshift plywood walls. We stepped up into the kitchen, where the abuela, standing in a bra and cotton shorts, cooks rice and beans and chicken. Another bedroom beside the kitchen. Open with no walls. The abuela's husband, the girl, the girl's sister, and a child-aunt all sit on the bed. The boss begins to explain in her learned campesino Spanish, as she sits down in the chair a young boy brings for her. She is comfortable in the home, with these strangers. Yes, you can take her, the abuela says, but she's a child. The results must be wrong. It's not possible.

A car ride into the city. The girl and her older sister in the backseat with us strangers in the front. The fever is gone, but her eyelids are swollen and her eyes watery. I wonder if that is how they always are. I ask if she wants a piece of gum. I ask her what grade she's in. Who her teacher is. She gives quiet one-word answers. We arrive. They take blood. Fifteen minutes later they know. It is true. The girl is HIV positive.

Her name is Laticia. She is eleven.

4.

What I come to know:

Her mother died a year ago. No one's sure from what.

She lives in a home with her abuela's ten children, plus her sister and two cousins.

Her stepfather and uncle also tested positive.

She has never met her father and does not know his name.

Sometimes her classmates make fun of her, calling her Haitiano because of her beautiful, rich, chocolate-colored skin. She was born here, and so was her mother.

5.

Another car ride into the city. Another blood test to do cell counts. Ten days later we return to get the results. Anemia. They cannot start the treatment. Thirty days of iron pills, and then we should return.

We sit in an empty classroom at the Center, a bowl of beads in front of us on the table. She strings the beads slowly as I explain that the necklace is going to remind her to take her pill every day. To start a habit so that it will be easier when the treatment begins. She picks out the glittery gold and silver beads. And the white hearts. She begins to talk. I've been told she knows what is going on from the doctors and the counselors. Other than the pills we do not talk about her sickness.

She comes to the Center every morning to take the pill. Each morning her necklace of beads is strung in a new pattern.

6.

Where did she get this? Does it matter? We think (hope) she was born with it. Can it be possible for a child to live for eleven years with the virus and no treatment and still be alive? Doubt creeps in. Do I want to think about other scenarios? Do we have the means to deal with other scenarios?

7.

A phone call from the clinic in the city. They have special doctors coming. Can we bring Laticia tomorrow? I cannot go, but Lucy goes in my place. Laticia has taken to her.

They return with news that she has eight cavities, and two extremely infected ears. I never heard her complain. Has she been living with pain her whole life? They offer a schedule of medicines—eardrops, cough syrup, children's Motrin—to be administered three times a day.

8.

I have come to check in on how taking the medicine is going. It has become time-consuming and Lucy and I are taking turns. Laticia's eighteen-year-old uncle lies in a beach chair in the front room. Femur broken. Face stitched up. Combination of alcohol, a moto bought with money won from a windsurfing championship, and a parked car. You will be the one who takes me over there. You're going to be my girlfriend and take me to the States, he says. There is no cast on his leg. Still two more months until it heals. Two more months of lying in that beach chair.

9.

She asks if she can come over to my house for lunch. Of course, I say. We have been spending a lot of time together, mostly reading. I cook up some spaghetti and she explores my place with her eyes. Taking in my Red Sox hat and my family pictures and the green troll on the table. I dish up the pasta and sit next to her. We've known each other for a month now.

Do you know what your sickness is? I ask her. She shakes her head no. You have no idea even what it's called? She shakes her head no. I pull out a piece of notebook paper and write "VIH" on it. What it stands for. What the words mean. What it does to your immune system, your body. How you get it. How you transfer it to others. How you treat it. And how, if she takes these pills called antiretrovirals, she can live a long, long life. She looks overwhelmed. Her swollen eyelids and teary eyes come back. We hug.

10.

When she falls in love and wants to share herself with someone, this conversation will always have to precede it. Will she find a moment of passion without worrying about passing on the virus? When she wants children, the egg must be fertilized without passing the virus on to her lover. That is not even an option for her in this place. If she does get pregnant, will she be with child without constantly worrying about passing the virus to her unborn baby?

11.

She's HIV positive, I say, knowing I do not have to, but as a courtesy, I guess. They are an American-run ministry clinic, and I know they'll do a good job. Lucy takes Laticia to the clinic. The dentist looks inside her gaping mouth. Yup, eight cavities. Awkwardness and hushed conversations. She's a child, they say; we're worried how she'll react to the anesthesia. You should take her to a pediatric orthodontist, where it might be better. This is a delicate situation, you understand. We do not want to make you upset. Read: She is HIV positive and the dentist will not work on her.

Understood, Lucy snaps.

That night Lucy replays the conversation in her head. We stare at each other across my kitchen table, a little red-eyed. This is a reality we know of, but we did not know.

12.

Go bathe, her abuela says. They forgot about the appointment and she isn't ready. She looks at me through glassy eyes. Her shoulders are stooped. Her arms hang. Slowly, she lugs the bucket of water to the back of the house, and pours it on herself in a less than private place. Sick and no privacy. No quiet. No solitude.

She comes back looking the same, same clothes, same hairdo except glistening from wetness. She walks closely to people as she makes her way to the car, like all she wants is someone to touch her. Perhaps in reassurance.

That evening Laticia started taking her antiretrovirals.

Community College

TIM BASCOM

Writing this time-lapse essay, which appeared in Witness, *was somewhat of a revelation for Tim Bascom. "Creative nonfiction swerves toward introspection," he says. "I'm glad that this essay focuses outward instead. It's still a bit of a surprise, since I am inclined the other way. Somehow, though, I kept the lens aimed away and learned in the process that I don't have to build an essay on self-reference."*

Week 1
Larry can't come because he went to his dad's place and found him on the floor, facedown, dead. Dwayne can't come because he's got black lung from smoking cigarettes. Mindy can't come because Wal-Mart changed her schedule; it's either eat or learn.

Week 2
Dwayne and Mindy are back, but Larry still can't come because of his dad's funeral.

Amanda is here, and she wants to talk. She's upset because, well, it's embarrassing, but after Blake asked her out and she said no, he sent her a nasty e-mail saying he had seen her on the Internet having sex. He's telling other people. She knows because a friend told her. She doesn't want people talking. Even if she did do that stuff, it's none of his business.

Week 3

Larry is back, but he may have to miss class once more so he can talk to the lawyer about his father's estate. His dad owned Larry's house. Now the sister wants to sell it. For her it's money; for him, it's where he lives.

Amanda is here, along with Blake, but they keep mouthing messages across the room.

Jane is here, as well, even though her daughter is struggling and her husband, a trucker, is away. She wants to write about the guy who came around selling insurance, the one who thought she shouldn't have painted her hallway like a U.S. flag. Where does he get off telling her what might upset people? If he doesn't like it, he can go back to India, or wherever he came from.

Week 4

Arlene can't come because she's attending a one-week course for beauticians. Nikki can't come because she's cutting herself, at least according to her friend. And John can't make it because he's in the psych ward.

Dwayne's gone, too—in the hospital—because the black lung turned to pneumonia. He'll be back, he whispers on the phone. He knows he's here for a reason; otherwise he'd be dead. He's been stabbed and shot, and almost died from the bad lungs, but God won't let him go. Jesus has a plan.

Oh, and Sara can't make it because she's got a migraine. They dilated her eyes, so it hurts to read.

Week 5

Jane is on time, as usual, but she looks frustrated. She isn't going to write about that guy who criticized her hallway walls. Who cares? He can go back to Saudi Arabia or wherever he's from. She's going to write about her first husband—because he was an addict and she didn't think her kids knew until she was at a pizza place and the littlest one got scared by a man at the next table. Her daughter said the man was a druggie. "How can you tell?" Jane asked. "Cause he has eyes like Daddy."

Week 6

Larry is back. He argued with his sister in the parking lot, so the estate isn't settled.

John is back, too, released from the psych ward. He says in high school he was a star on the football team and got good grades—before the army put him in a morgue where he had to look at bodies from Iraq. He says he can make up all the work now, if he can find his books.

Week 7

Dan's been coming every day, despite his diabetes. His sight is getting worse, but he can still use the computer. He types his notes big—about two inches tall—and if he pulls at the corners of his eyes, he can read.

Jimmy is here all the time, too, and he smiles. He says he didn't used to be so easygoing, not until the skull fracture. His parents aren't so sure about the change, but he's happy. He thinks he used to cause too much trouble. He grins when he describes the extreme kickboxing that he does to make money on the side. The best way to win, he explains, is to hurt the other guy in a leg.

Week 8—Midterm

Arlene has disappeared, never to return from the beautician's course. And Chase is gone, even though his first paper (about body piercing) was beautiful. Mindy is AWOL as well, after coming back long enough to explain that she's not sure if she's a lesbian—which, along with the Wal-Mart work schedule, is making it hard for her to get anything done.

Amanda is back, but she doesn't want to press Blake on the Internet thing. There's something she should have explained—because actually she *is* on the Internet. It was one of those webcam things, and there's lots of others involved. She didn't think anyone here would see it.

Dwayne is back, too. The pneumonia is over, but now he doesn't care about anything. His woman friend says she can't see him since she isn't divorced. It doesn't make sense: if she loves him, then why doesn't she want to see him? He can feel himself going hard inside like he used to get before he went to prison. He wants to feel that way again so it doesn't hurt. If God gave him this woman, then why take her away?

Week 9

Sara has another migraine, so she can't make it. Heather can't be here because her fiancé is returning from Iraq for the wedding. Nikki can't be here because she has been cutting herself again, according to her friend, who says that once, in grade school, Nikki convinced a boy to break her arm.

Clarissa isn't coming either. She won't say why, but her brother, Ronnie, thinks she's depressed. As for Ronnie, he comes all the time, despite the fact that he was born with spina bifida and had fifteen surgeries on his legs and has to use a wheelchair.

Week 10

Dan is on time as usual, with his cane in hand and his bad eyes up to the computer. He is applying for a scholarship for the blind, so he can get into computer programming at the university. He wants to know if he will get his paper back. Last year the woman in charge never gave papers back. Not even on the last day. He doesn't want an A if he didn't earn it.

Larry is coming regularly, too, although his dad's estate is in stalemate. He says he will have to miss class once more when he goes to court with his ex. He doesn't like the essay about how women get marked—Miss, Mrs., and Ms. "Men get marked, too," he says. "Men are always at fault. Go to court and you'll see."

Dwayne is still coming, but he doesn't know why. His woman friend won't see him, and he can't stand the apartment. It reminds him of the way his dad used to put him in the garage and make him sleep there.

Week 11

For the first time, Jane is absent. She drops by to apologize. She has discovered that her junior high–age daughter stole $1,000 out of the ATM machine to give to a girl who keeps kicking her after school. There was a note in her daughter's drawer explaining why she might kill herself. Jane's sorry to be late, but she had to talk to the principal. If he won't do anything, she's going to press charges.

John hasn't made up any of his missed work, and he is not answering e-mails. Mindy isn't answering e-mails either. And now William is missing because he has rehearsals for the community play, *Julius Caesar*. He's playing a commoner, he says in his message. "Hey, like real life!" he adds.

Week 12

Dan is here as usual, but he says he will have to leave halfway through. He's still putting together the scholarship application—the one for blind students—but he can't stay because there's been some trouble at home. Family first, you know.

Nikki is back, too, and she wants to write about people who cut themselves.

Jimmy is smiling like usual, but he announces that he will take next semester off. He's going to stop the extreme kickboxing. They don't pay enough to cover injuries. Instead, he's going to be a bounty hunter in Chicago, going after guys who skip bail. There's a device to help him see into a room. That's the main thing—to see inside before you knock down the door.

Amanda hasn't come for weeks. She sends e-mails to explain. She's sorry about the whole Blake-Internet-sex thing. But she's got her act together now—because she has joined the army. After a year at a fort in Texas, she'll ship out to Iraq. It will be tough on her family, she knows. Especially her two-year-old. But she's not worried because the girl will be in good hands.

Week 13

Sara is back. The migraines are over. She wants to write about mules because she has one at home. They're not stubborn, she says. They're smart.

Mindy is back, too, after two weeks AWOL. She says she doesn't want to talk about it, but then she does anyway. A guy friend raped her, and she couldn't come to class because she had a black eye. She hasn't told her parents because her dad might do something stupid. She says this isn't helping with the whole lesbian deal, or the job at Wal-Mart.

Week 14

Jane has turned in her paper about the ex-husband who's an addict, and she's proud of it. She says her junior high daughter is doing much better now that the other girl isn't kicking her.

Blake has turned in his paper also (about hunting for turkeys), but it's word-for-word from a site on the Internet. So's Amanda's paper, which she e-mailed from where she is getting trained as a soldier. After she learns that she has been caught, she e-mails back to say she's sorry. She feels just terrible. Since she doesn't deserve to take classes, she's going to drop them all.

Sara turns in her paper about mules, and she's right: they're smart.

Week 15

Maxine will have to miss the last two weeks because she's getting her stomach stapled.

John, who has been released from the psych ward for the second time, says he is going to let this semester ride. He'll try again after the meds are adjusted.

Mindy wants an extension, so she can make up the missing paper after she works through the rape and the whole lesbian issue.

Nikki turns in her paper late—the one about people who cut themselves—and it's a fine bit of writing. Still, she says, she's not going to take classes anymore. Her friend explains: "She's pregnant. The guy's a jerk."

Larry gets his paper in late, too. He says it's okay to dock it. He understands. Anyway, he doesn't know if he'll be back. The lawyer told him he might have to sell his house. How's he going to finish his degree if he's homeless?

Week 16—Finals Week

Jimmy comes by on the last day of the semester, just to say bye. He says he learned a lot. He says he'll be back if the bounty hunter deal doesn't pan out.

Dan drops by, too, when everyone else has gone. He holds out a letter from the university. It says he got the scholarship. He is full of thanks. Thanks for the letter of reference and the advice about the application. Thanks for helping to make it happen. His eyes are pale. They focus on nothing. He shifts the cane to his left hand and reaches with his right. He doesn't want to hear about how he did all the work himself, or how he deserves the money. His grip is firm.

Cantata 147: The Final Chorale

AMY ANDREWS

Amy Andrews compares the process of composition to quilt-making: "When I am writing an essay," she says, "I often find myself holding a block of memory, or a fact, in my hands, and considering its lightness or its darkness. I play with it, spinning it in its place, pairing it, or repositioning it completely to another quadrant of the essay. Squinting, I try to glimpse the quieter patterns that seem always just beyond my knowing."

Any one who has common sense will remember that the bewilderments of the eyes are of two kinds, and arise from two causes, either from coming out of the light or from going into the light, which is true of the mind's eye, quite as much as of the bodily eye; and he who remembers this when he sees any one whose vision is perplexed and weak, will not be too ready to laugh; he will first ask whether that

185

soul of man has come out of the brighter light,
and is unable to see because unaccustomed to
the dark, or having turned from darkness to
the day is dazzled by excess of light.

—Plato, *The Republic*

When I was in high school, I would let off the accelerator, just a bit, whenever I drove past the little street not far from the intersection of Floyd and Campbell roads where Mr. Hargrove used to live. I'd study the humble houses, lined up as soldiers might be under the scorching Texas heat, and try to find a house that looked different from all the others. I'd look for a house where the lawn looked somewhat less groomed, a house where the paint seemed a bit faded, where cars gathered at the curb. I'd try to find a house that gave a clue, however small, that it was the sort of house you might drive up to and press the garage door operator and find your husband, or your father, swinging from a rope.

But they all looked the same to me. The houses were equally silent, equally still. Shrubs trimmed, lawns edged, walks swept, the neighborhood always seemed uniformed, at attention. Any, all, evidence of desperation or disaster, erased.

MR. HARGROVE WAS my band director during my middle school years. On one level his job was a straightforward one: instructing large groups of awkward, squirming pre-adolescent students armed with noise-making devices in the principles of music performance. Never mind that we brought varying degrees of interest and talent to the project. Some of us lacked a sense of rhythm, and most of us suffered from profound insensitivity to pitch. We invariably found the dramas large and small that occurred in the hallways before band and after band more compelling, their effect far more concentrated in our hearts and our stomachs, than the most eloquent orchestrations of black notes on white paper. We were in band because it filled space, in our schedules and in our lives, in a way that was more engaging than, say, study hall.

Which makes the fact that Mr. Hargrove was able to extract award-winning performances from similar gatherings of students year in and year out all the more extraordinary. Indeed, our school district had become rather well known for its exceptional band program, and I think we knew, somehow, that when we entered the hallowed, pale blue band hall, we were inheritors of a noble tradition. Whatever we may have lacked in talent and even interest must have been balanced by skillful instruction and pride in this tradition.

I remember Mr. Hargrove as a handsome man with chiseled features, tousled hair, deep eyes, and an easy smile who, in spite of his warm and kind demeanor, always seemed to be somehow of another place. He wore glasses that darkened with the light and combined with his brown vinyl coat to give him a hip look that seemed ever so slightly out of step with our other teachers and drew our admiration. He was not shy about telling us he played the cornet outside of school, beyond band, before band and after band, in jazz ensembles and in bars, in places poorly lit and smoky. When he'd borrow a horn to demonstrate a melody, I remember watching his eyes close and sensing that he left us, just for a moment, whenever he played.

He was the sort of man a girl of twelve or thirteen or fourteen might have studied from her place in the flute section, from just below his podium and to his left, watching him when he was completely unaware of being watched, wondering what he might have been like to kiss. And when he'd borrow one of our flutes in service of instruction, we'd make faces at each other and feign disgust at the prospect of finding remnants of his saliva in our instruments. We never spoke to each other of how his lips looked spread out warm and soft on our mouthpieces or of how it felt, when he handed our instruments back to us, to hold his breath, still warm and damp, in the hollows of our gleaming silver wands.

> *I remember that you kindly condescended to ask for some news of my fate; this shall now most obediently be done. The vicissitudes from my youth on are well known to you, as far as the change that took me to Cothen as director of music. There I had a gracious prince who loved music as much as he knew it, and I thought that I would end my career at his court. But . . . the said prince married a princess of Berenburg, and it began to seem as if his musical leanings grew lukewarm, chiefly because the new princess seemed to be rather empty-headed. So God willed that my vocation should be that of musical director and CANTOR at the Thomasschule here, although in truth, initially I found it difficult to envisage being changed from a director of music into a cantor. So I put off making my decision for three months. However, the post was described to me in such glowing terms that finally (particularly because it seemed favourable to my sons' studies) I decided in the name of God to travel to Leipzig, go through the audition and, in the end, move. Here, by the will of God, I still am. However, since 1) I find the post much less desirable than it had been described to me, 2) many perquisites due to me in my situation are denied to me, 3) it is very expensive here and 4) those over me are capricious and have little feeling for music so I have to live in almost continuous frustration, envy and persecution, I perceive that, with the aid of the Almighty, I must seek elsewhere for my fortune . . .*

Johann Sebastian Bach

28 October 1730

Bach wrote to Georg Erdmann, Russian consul in Gdansk, after seven years as the Cantor in Leipzig. He was looking for a way out, for relief from almost unbearable circumstances. He endured rooms "cold, dark, dank and unsanitary," taught students who were "undisciplined scoundrels," and directed singers and performers who were "grossly incompetent."[1] And he had an unbearable boss who tried to humiliate him at every turn. Burdened with mundane responsibilities— morning prayers, evening prayers, meal supervision, visits to the sanatorium, "seeing that the boys came back from weddings and funerals in a sober and orderly manner"—he wanted only music.

But even in Leipzig there had been a beginning. There had been a glowing and hopeful time, early months full of enthusiasm and promise, and it was in this time that Bach composed the final chorale to Part I of Cantata 147, "Herz und Mund und Tat und Leben" ("Heart and mouth, deeds and life"). He wove it of old threads, threads handed down by men he probably never knew, strophs of a hymn sixty years old, lines of a melody eighty years old. To these worn and would-be forgotten bits Bach added his own special genius for hearing the way voices high and low and in between might bounce off of each other, dancing over and under and around each other in elegant simplicity. "Jesu, Joy of Man's Desiring," the popularized title to this section of the cantata, was born of a hopeful time, a hopeful heart, before the grinding insults of the Thomasschule drove Bach to look for escape.

WHEN MR. HARGROVE passed around the music for "Jesu, Joy of Man's Desiring"—copies slightly aslant, edges scorched by the copy machine—we balanced the papers on teetering black music stands and groaned. The marks held nothing for us; they were just black notes on white paper, pieces of a puzzle for which we had neither understanding nor interest. We would have preferred something contemporary, jazzy, something with a groove, and we were surely unimpressed to learn that the music was hundreds of years old.

I don't remember playing the piece over and over; I don't remember which parts were difficult; I don't remember whether Ann

Pearson or Mira Sconzo or my best friend Jennifer or even I held first-chair flute position at the time. I remember only how we kept to the work of our triplets (tri-pe-let/tri-pe-let/tri-pe-let/tri-pe-let) while the horns and the oboes gently, insistently, lifted up a hidden melody, slower and smoother but no less joyful, from beneath. I remember the way Mr. Hargrove, paying only scant attention with his left hand to our dutiful tripleting, would stroke and smooth the sound coming from the horns with his right hand, singing with it, dancing with it, holding it in his arms, his eyes wide open and fixed on a point far away. I remember the delicate lines of sweat etched on the side of his temple.

It is the only song I remember playing in Concert Band. I'm sure there were others, but this is the one I remember. We played it at concerts for parents. We played it for judges at competition. We played it for the tape machine that recorded it for the album that now sits dusty and silent on a shelf with hundreds of other dusty and silent albums. And if we ever started loving the song, we certainly never confessed it to each other, much less to Mr. Hargrove.

Sometime during the last week of my ninth-grade year, Jennifer and I were intercepted by Mr. Hargrove in the band room. We'd not played under his direction for over a year, having been promoted to Mr. Arsers's Symphonic Band. But he had continued to be one star in that constellation of adults so important to adolescents—an adult who knew us by name, thought of us fondly, and stood between us and the darkness. He caught us as we were passing through the band hall, on the way to somewhere else, and he pulled us into his office to ask us to reconsider our decisions to forgo band at the high school. I'm sure we didn't mention the fact that people who played in the band at the high school were "band nerds." I'm sure I didn't offer that I would never do anything if Jennifer did not also do it. Instead we spoke of busy schedules, advanced courses, ballet lessons, piano lessons, jobs. I imagine we smiled demurely, flattered that he should care at all. And I'm sure we acted nonchalant when, just before we left, he placed his hands on our arms, just above the elbows, and, with a plaintive squeeze, said, "I just hate to see you close any doors on yourselves."

We left his office, and the pale blue band room, the imprint of his hand still tingling in our skin, his last words to us rocketing around in our ears.

HISTORIANS SCRATCH THEIR heads in wonder and amazement as they try to make sense of Bach's achievements. He was not, they point out, well-parented, well-educated, well-read, well-traveled, or well-spoken. Nor was he well-received in his time. One critic wrote: "That some of the noblest and most-majestic music ever conceived by man should have come from one of such limited intelligence and experience—and from one continually burdened and harassed by taxing and ungratifying work schedules—is one of the great paradoxes of art." Bach's only explanation: "I worked hard."

But historians seem to find this explanation incomplete. They look for connections between the apparently devout Lutheran life Bach led and the unspeakably grand and majestic music he composed. Some scholars believe the connection is tenuous at best, that Bach's use of religious texts and themes was nothing more than a nod to the conventions of his era. Others insist, "there is in the music profound mystical intensity that could only have come from the spirit of a man who was moved to the uttermost of his being." They wonder whether Bach's music is strictly the work of an astute and technically gifted composer, or if it is better understood as testament of a miraculous and profound faith, echoes of a reverent communion with God. They agree only on the fact that we will never know, can never know for sure, the intensity of a man's faith. And we can never know if it is Bach's voice, or God's, singing still.

———

IF WE THOUGHT little of God when we played "Jesu, Joy of Man's Desiring" for Mr. Hargrove, we pondered God's relevance more directly when, a few months after exiting the band room, we joined hundreds of others in the sanctuary pews facing his casket at the altar. The organist played "Jesu," and we mouthed the words to the hymn for the first time, surprised, even embarrassed, to realize the music we had played under more secular circumstances originated in the sacred:

> *Jesu, joy of our desiring,*
> *Holy wisdom, love most bright*
> *Drawn by thee, our souls aspiring,*
> *Soar to uncreated light . . .*
>
> *Word of God, our flesh that fashioned,*
> *With the fire of life impassioned*
> *Striving still to truth unknown,*
> *Soaring, dying round thy throne . . .*
>
> *Through the way where hope is guiding,*
> *Hark, what peaceful music rings!*
> *Where the flock, in Thee confiding,*
> *Drink of joy from deathless springs.*
>
> *Theirs is beauty's fairest pleasure;*
> *Theirs is wisdom's holiest treasure.*
> *Thou dost ever lead Thine own*
> *In the love of joys unknown.*

We sang these words, our eyes fixed on the open casket at the altar rail. We felt, if we did not understand, the steady procession of the music, the rhythmic trochees landing line after line on definitive spondees. But I doubt we contemplated, as I do now, the dark edges of such a passion. How words of such adoration and longing, words that plead for nearness—intimacy, even union—might court a desperate man. And sometimes I wonder whether this is a faith more likely to forestall—or hasten—the orchestration of a death.

No one knew, and there was no explaining what happened. My mother told me he had just received a promotion, had just been asked to conduct the bands at the high school. Other parents marveled at what appeared to be a strong family life, a loving wife and a thriving little boy. They shook their heads in disbelief and said he had it all.

Frightened, we filled in the gaps with suppositions. In low whispers, after the funeral, there was speculation about financial difficulties, or an illness. Perhaps some unseen professional disappointment, or disillusionment, some dream unrealized. Perhaps an affair. Any explanation more plausible than the thought that a handsome man full of music and humor, a man we'd looked up to and admired, a man who had loved us and cared for us even when we had braces and pimples and poor manners and fragile hearts, could secretly harbor such desperation. Anything but the fact that an emptiness so terrifying had moved and breathed in our midst, its lips on our flutes, its hand on our arms, pleading and undetected.

BACH NEVER LEFT Leipzig. He stayed on at the Thomasschule for twenty years after writing to Erdmann, in the same dark rooms, under the same working conditions, composing nevertheless "a library of music incomparable for its majesty and grandeur." And in his later years, he underwent two operations, both unsuccessful, to hold on to his failing eyesight. The light, he said, caused him pain. After the operations, Bach went completely blind, but nevertheless worked feverishly for another year, dictating, in the darkness, canons and fugues and chorales such as "When We In Sorest Trouble Are."

Ten days before he died, his sight returned. He could behold the faces of his seventeen children, his wife, his music. He could see clearly, sharply. How bright and jarring might the world have seemed? How unnatural—or glorious—the light?

What drives some men to make music of the darkness while other men cinch it around their necks and suffocate in it? I wonder about these things whenever I am driving in my car from here to there, hurrying to get somewhere else, or to become someone else, and the radio calls me back. The oboes and horns of "Jesu" rise up beneath my hurried tripletingtripletingtripleting and remind me how handsome, how alive, how holy Mr. Hargrove looked whenever we played for him, with his chin lifted to the light, his glasses darkened, his eyes closed. And I regret that I never summoned the language, or the courage, to tell him how Bach's music felt, braided and beautiful and breathing in my body, even then. But mostly the music haunts me, recalls the memory of how beautiful, alive, and holy he looked in his casket, composed and still, the undertaker having succeeded in covering whatever marks the rope may have left on his neck, the lines from here to there still so invisible, so unfathomable, and so easily erased.

[1]This and following quotations from David Ewen, ed., *Great Composers 1300–1900: A Biographical and Critical Guide* (New York: H. W. Wilson Company, 1966).

I Can't Answer

Spade's a Spade, or The Burden of Being Right (open.salon.com)

> There are blows in life so violent—
> I can't answer!
>
> —César Vallejo

I turned twenty-two on a Saturday, graduated Stanford Sunday afternoon, and that evening caught a red-eye to Houston and then a cab that got me to the brick school in the ghetto at eight-fifteen, just slightly late. I hadn't slept. The room was full of young, bleary-eyed men and women dressed professionally in collared shirts and belted slacks. The warm air smelled of deodorant and coffee. Everyone stared as I lowered myself to a child's chair with a complaint of plastic. The black woman in the pantsuit resumed speaking where she'd left off, her voice thick with conviction.

"You do not understand the poverty these children come from, their single-parent families. They will bring their circumstances to the classroom, where it is your job to offer them opportunity. You will think you know what they need. You will not."

I had a hard time focusing; I could see the woman's lips moving, but found the words made little sense. It was fine: ethnic studies had taught me all about poverty and inequality, and I knew all about the struggle of students of color. This woman cited no statistics or numbers, but went on and on about children she'd taught, their struggles and suffering. After the session, I wrote on my evaluation card: "Presentation was lacking in sufficient intellectual content."

Darnisha was easy to dislike. She was chubby-cheeked and had perfect caramel skin—the lightest girl in the class, and so the envy of all the rest. She came to school made up, eye-makeup and blush on a fourth grader, and she wore pleated skirts and blouses with ruffles, not fading polos and hand-me-down khakis wearing at the knees like the other kids. Her hair was always pulled in fresh braids or rows, with different colored bands and balls that matched the color of the uniform. Her bag was Hello Kitty and I disliked the brightness of the pink, the white trim unstained, as if someone laundered it each day. Her pencils weren't yellow but blue and green inlaid with silver and gold stars and tiny, smiling animals. She spoke with a bubbly, forward-rushing energy, always hurrying to the next bright, happy thing.

"My mama say I can be anything I want, and I want to do everything, everything," she'd say.

"Well, you may have to choose one or two 'things,' " I'd say, cautioning her against diffuse aspirations. Here her classmates had screamed going over the one-story highway overpass on our way to a play in Greenwood—they had never been so high. Darnisha had been astonished, then told them about staying on the thirtieth floor of the Hilton in Memphis, the walls all "glass, glass, glass and them bright city lights."

"How many 'glasses' was there? Or did you mean 'windows'?" Felicia, my sharp-tongued favorite, cut in derisively while Darnisha wilted. I ought to have interceded, but pretended not to have heard. It wasn't just that Darnisha's parents had money, her mother a nurse at the hospital in Greenville and her father—she had a father, which was in itself an oddity—a contractor. It was the way she flaunted what she had, showing off her new leather shoes to an adoring crowd of girls wearing latex Wal-Mart knockoffs, basking in her plenty, boasting about her trips to Jackson and Memphis and the deep blue swimming pools and all-you-can-eat buffets in the resort-casinos of Tunica and Biloxi. It was the way the kids kowtowed to her, not resentful but admiring of her air of bounty.

I especially hated the way she moved. She was sleek and big-bodied like a seal, had this way of applauding her own arrival, clasping her hands and breathlessly announcing what she'd done, what she was thinking, what she was going to do next. Some days, watching her in class, I would find myself frowning at her. Other times, I'd pass her upraised hand for a second or third time, hoping for anyone else with an answer. She was bright and curious and courteous, less of a problem than the rest of my motley crew with their clamor and defiance and rejecting disinterest. Really, she was the model student. She just didn't need me—she would have been fine in any classroom, in any place, the statistics said. Children of stable, middle-class, two-parent households were well enough off anywhere.

Each afternoon at three-fifteen, Darnisha's father picked her up, pulled his white Ford 150 up to the gates of the school and rolled down the tinted windows and called, "Come on, baby," in his booming voice while the other children looked on. I'd wave to him, as masculine a wave as I could manage—I was never at ease with black men, who always towered over me. When she was gone I'd feel a sense of relief, would take the three or four kids who remained back to the classroom, where they'd stay until five and six o'clock in the sanctuary of my room, away from the dusty streets and grassed lots, the ball court with its cracked cement and the old men who lingered in the shade, backs leaned to the chain-link fence watching with hungry eyes. Those kids had no other retreat, no air-conditioned cab and waiting father and home with their own bedroom. They sat in my room, talked sometimes about Darnisha and what her papa has, what she have and do, without jealousy. They harbored only a pure and impossible longing to be her.

I tried to be kind because she liked me. One day in early October Darnisha spent all day beaming at me, finally came to me after the bell. "Mr. Copperman, it National Teacher 'Preciation day, so my mama sent you some apples."

"Appreciation," I corrected.

She held out a white bag with a bow containing a half-dozen red and orange streaked Gala apples, marked with stickers saying "Washington." They had to be from the Kroger in Greenville, thirty miles away—the Sunflower food store in Indianola carried only pale, mealy Granny Smiths.

"Thanks," I said.

When she was gone, I gave the apples to the children who were still in the classroom. "Man, these apples sweet. Sure you don't want none, Mr. Copperman?" Andrea said with her mouth full of Gala.

I shook my head. I wanted no part of what Darnisha had.

One afternoon Darnisha's father hadn't arrived at three-fifteen. We stood at the gates to the school, sweating in the sun and listening for the sound of his pickup, and finally I gave up and took Andrea and her brother, Tyrone, back to the classroom with Darnisha in tow. Her father knew where my room was. The kids were happy to have Darnisha there, especially Andrea, the poorest girl in the class, whom I'd often seen admiring Darnisha from afar. Andrea's uniform shirts were holed and stained, and often she and her brother reeked of sweat, their clothes not washed for a month and they unshowered because their water was turned off at home. Andrea and Darnisha were in the same guided reading group, which was on the third Harry Potter book, and they discussed the intrigue and fun of it, their favorite part of all that magic. "I like how they live there in those big rooms with beds and got spells to bring as much as they want fresh and hot to that big dinner table," Andrea said.

"I just love love love how they go to that dark wood and it so scary but they always come back fine," Darnisha said.

Love, love, love, I thought as I pushed open the classroom door and set the children to tasks, Andrea and Darnisha filing papers and wiping the chalkboard while little Tyrone vacuumed the reading rug. I had to keep an eye on Tyrone—sometimes things disappeared in his pockets, though I didn't blame him. I'd passed their house, the porch sagging to the dirt yard, the walls and roof bowing toward the center, and the broken-out windows covered in black plastic. If I were him I'd take what I could get.

The children finished their tasks, got more. The minutes passed. Darnisha became a bit anxious, and I assured her that her father was surely on his way. At four-thirty the secretary appeared in my door, her mouth pressed in a line. She beckoned me into the hall, spoke in a whisper. "That girl Darnisha's father wrapped his pickup 'bout a pole on the highway. He ain't—he passed. Y'all gone have to wait for the girl mother come pick her up."

My breath left my chest. "Oh, God." I felt an awful, guilty slide: what had I wished on her? I glanced back in the room. All of them were staring with the child's instinct for trouble.

"Thank you," I said to the secretary. "I'll stay here until you call."

I went back in the room, went to Andrea and Tyrone and put my hands to their shoulders. "It's time for the two of you to leave," I said. Andrea nodded, and the two of them grabbed their backpacks and went without protest, fleeing what had closed suddenly about the room. I shut the door behind them. Darnisha stood alone, her eyes wild. "What it is, Mr. Copperman? What she say? Where my papa is? Where?"

I stood with lips working, stricken, not wanting to tell her of the sorrow she was bound for, and no excuse I could make. Just moments before, I had despised the way her mouth turned up, the shine of her teeth, the dimples in her pudgy little-girl cheeks. And now, here I was with her. Here, and no words sufficient for grief.

An Open Letter

FIRST DRAFT: LAYING DOWN THE WORDS
(KATHYRHODES.WORDPRESS.COM)

My Dear Husband,

I need to clear the air. I have regrets, guilt, and I need to talk to you about it. I went to a grief counselor and it was recommended that I write you a letter and say what I want to say and then perhaps burn the letter and take the ashes with yours to the Tennessee River beside Neyland Stadium and send them off with you. But I'm keeping you here with me until I resolve my guilt and I'm ready to release you. And I'm saying this openly because I suspect there is a community of us who are caught up in living and don't grasp that we are walking a tightrope between life and death, and then when death comes suddenly, it catches us wishing we'd done it all differently, and it heaps loads of guilt on our backs. What we do with our guilt affects how we grieve and heal. I suspect I will always hold myself somewhat accountable. You were mine to take care of, and I didn't do a good job. We both knew that you were the caregiver in our relationship, but that doesn't excuse my actions on that fateful day.

First of all, I'm so sorry I didn't follow my gut feelings. A couple of weeks before you died, I remember looking at you one evening as you sat in your chair watching *Larry King Live* or one of those Lifetime movies you hated, and what I saw made me gush aloud with no tact because it was so vividly blatant. "My gosh, your face is gray and chalky. What's wrong with you?" You were not happy with my observation. "Nothing," you said, taken aback, "I'm fine." But on subsequent nights, I stole glances at you and you had that same grayish and whitish look and not the pinkish red face I was used to seeing. Maybe this was a sign of the catastrophic event that ultimately took your life. Maybe not. Maybe I should have insisted you go to the doctor. Maybe you'd be alive today if I had. We're talking about your life here, and I didn't do enough to save it. I'm so sorry.

A week before you died, you looked at me one evening and rubbed your legs together and said, "My legs are tingling." I knew with those words that something was wrong with you. Maybe then I should have insisted that you go to the doctor. Maybe you'd be alive today if I had. I'm so sorry. But I know as well as I know my own name that the doctor wouldn't have suspected aortic dissection. After all, many people have tingling legs. My father did all his adult life. He rubbed his legs together like a cricket and complained every night. He lived to be eighty-four and didn't die like you did.

I remember you telling me that your back hurt. "Low back?" I asked. "No," you said, "between my shoulder blades." Your olive green eyes looked into mine, wanting an answer. You'd never hurt there. Now I suspect it was caused by the aneurysm or tear, or the process of aortic dissection beginning. I couldn't have known, but I wish I'd done something to stop that horrific process. After all, it was your life. I'm so sorry.

I always teased and told you I knew everything and I could diagnose your aches and pains, but when it really mattered, I didn't know anything, and I couldn't diagnose you, and I couldn't take care of you, and I didn't, and I'm so sorry. I've spent my entire life trying to make things all right, and I couldn't make this all right.

I keep thinking back to that Friday morning, a little over a month ago. You woke up at three, sick. You didn't wake me then, but told me at five, when I got up. You just told me you had diarrhea. I thought you had a stomach virus, or maybe salmonella from the tomatoes we had eaten. You thought so, too. I was a little miffed with you because in your job you were always touching people's mice and keyboards and catching things, even though you used Purell religiously. I even tried to stay away from you because in two days, I was leaving for Asheville to be with Son #2 while he had an endoscopy for a persistent problem, a feeling like something was in his throat. He had convinced himself he had esophageal cancer and had me worried, too. I couldn't go to this procedure if I caught a stomach virus. I sprayed the house with Lysol and regret this display of drama. I'm so sorry I didn't put my arms around you and my face against yours and hold you and ask what I could do to help. Instead, I worked with a vengeance that morning. I paid bills, I did invoices for Genisys, I went to the bank, I went to Publix to get you crackers and ginger ale—my God, you could have died while I was gone!—I tried to complete all my work so I could be gone a few days. I didn't know how serious it was, I didn't know how incredibly sick you were, and I'm so sorry.

You didn't tell me there was blood with the diarrhea, and lots of it, until later in the morning. I called the doctor, but by then the staff was at lunch. "Let's just be there at 1:30 when they get back," I said. "Or do you think this is an emergency and we should go on to the hospital?" You said it would be 1:30 before you could get your clothes on anyway. As we drove up under the canopy, you said you'd need a wheelchair. "Really?" I said. I still wasn't understanding how sick you were. I got a nurse and we wheeled you in.

I knew it was something bad when you told the doctor that it felt like someone had jabbed a broom handle down your throat. You hadn't told me that, and I keep seeing the image of you illustrating that to the doctor. He wrote up orders to admit you to the hospital, and I wheeled you back out to the car. "Okay, get up and get in the car," I said. You didn't move. I didn't realize you couldn't move. "C'mon," I said, patting you, then trying to hold your arm and help you. You looked around at me with twitchy movements, and I'm not sure if you were passing out or seizing or what, but I remember shaking your shoulder and yelling, "Stay with me, Charlie! Don't you leave me!" I ran inside for help. A doctor and nurse came running outside. I told her to call 911, which she did. A team took you inside and put you on a table and held your legs up and I helped them and they started an IV and tried to stabilize you. Every doctor and nurse in the place was working on you. The ambulance arrived and took you away, and I was scared out of my mind, but I still didn't know how sick you were, and I'm so sorry. I called my sons, I called my friend Currie, I hurried to the ER.

They kept your IV going, they started giving you blood, you screamed with pain and writhed and pulled out all your tubes, and they couldn't give you anything for pain because your BP was so low they couldn't even get a reading except by Doppler. You said, "It's bad isn't it?" and I should have said yes, but all I did was try and calm you. I thought they could correct your problem with surgery, I thought you'd be okay.

You wouldn't have wanted the five hours of surgery, the life flight to Vanderbilt, six more hours of surgery, then an additional hour of surgery, during which you succumbed. You always said you wanted to "go" quickly. You lived thirty-eight hours. It was a violently invasive thirty-eight hours, and I can't get over the catastrophic nature of it and never will. I'm so sorry you had to go through all that.

Most of all, I'm so sorry I took you to the doctor and you never got to come home again. Your life was full of loose ends. You never got to tell the dog good-bye. You had jobs for customers pending, inventory ordered. You had season tickets for UT football, hotel reservations made. You bought parts to fix the grill, you were going to fix the headlight on my car, you were going to clean the gutters out, and you wanted to buy a bicycle like mine, or a motorbike. It's like we were walking along having a normal life like everybody else and all of a sudden we were at the edge of a cliff, and this was truly where the world ended. Only it was you that fell off, and not me, and I'm so sorry it ended for you and it ended this way. And I want you to know it ended for me, too, in a different way.

Our wedding vows that we composed together concluded with "I want to endure all things with you. I want to walk home to God with you." You kept your promise to me. I cannot keep mine to you, and I'm so sorry.

In baring my innermost soul to the whole world, I am in hopes that others will remember my experience and ponder and prevent the likes from happening to them, the guilt and regrets part, that is. I am letting you know that I feel so unworthy to have had you, so undeserving of your goodness and generous spirit, so unworthy as a person. I am so sorry I didn't do better with what I had.

Yours,
Kathy

A Perfunctory Affair

Chris Cobb

"I think doing a lot of documentary photography led me to write creative nonfiction," says Chris Cobb. "In the process of making photographs at events it occurred to me that whatever narrative I created would be considered the 'true' narrative. . . . This is an interesting challenge—to select from all the information at one's disposal and to distill it down to just the bare essentials and still be accurate." This story about working on a 2008 Sol LeWitt installation appeared in The Believer.

> When an artist uses a conceptual form of art, it means that all of the planning and decisions are made beforehand and the execution is a perfunctory affair. The idea becomes a machine that makes the art.
>
> —"Paragraphs on Conceptual Art,"
> by Sol LeWitt, *Artforum*, June 1967

Lines of Human Convergence

When conceptual artist Sol LeWitt died, in 2007, at the age of seventy-eight, he was in the process of planning the last, and biggest, exhibition of his career—a wall-drawing retrospective at the Massachusetts Museum of Contemporary Art (MASS MoCA). The scale of the intended exhibition was humongous by any measure. One entire 27,000-square-foot Industrial Revolution–era factory building (MASS MoCA's Building 7) would house wall drawings spanning LeWitt's entire career, from 1968 until 2007. The final result would be an important scholarly resource, a reference point for all future LeWitt installations, and a major tourist draw to the small corner of western Massachusetts where MASS MoCA is located. Given its size, scope, and durability, what might have been just another blockbuster show would likely become one of the great art pilgrimages in the United States.

It was LeWitt's wish that the MASS MoCA team be made up of crew members who'd worked on his previous installations. So in early April 2008, about thirteen professional artists (of which I am one), nine apprentices, fourteen interns, and LeWitt's eight closest assistants converged on the town of North Adams. We'd all abandoned our jobs and our home lives in order to spend five months installing a total of one hundred wall drawings.

To give a broader sense of the installation's scale: the drawings we'd come to install would occupy nearly an acre of wall space. The estimated project budget was about 10 million dollars. It would take almost fifty people putting in eight-hour days, six days a week, from April to October, to complete the installation. Thousands of yards of red rosin paper were needed to cover the floors as we painted. Other supplies we required: hundreds of rolls of white receipt paper; brown roll paper in one-foot and half-foot widths; dozens of rulers; dozens of boxes of drafting tape in one-inch and half-inch widths;

dozens of boxes of blue masking tape, paper towels, and thin green tape; rolls of plastic sheeting; gallons and gallons of Benjamin Moore house paint in white, black, and gray; dozens of bottles of Lascaux acrylic paint in black, white, red, yellow, and blue; dozens of gallons of distilled water (for mixing with the Lascaux paint); more than a thousand water-soluble pastel crayons in white, red, yellow, and blue; dozens of paintbrushes in various sizes; several cases of large foam core board sheets; thousands of razor blades; lots of Spackle; many, many rolls of sheet plastic; dozens of paint trays and liners; paint rollers, stirring sticks, etc., etc., etc.

For the pencil drawings, red, blue, yellow, and graphite pencil leads were ordered (180,000 of each color). Once the project started, there would be up to three people a day doing nothing but sharpening pencil leads.

Wall Drawing #343

I'm in the middle of a fifty-seven-foot (and three-quarters-of-an-inch-long) wall, which itself is situated in the middle of a maze of walls on the second floor of Building 7. I am working, alongside my apprentice Julia, on Wall Drawing #343. By "working on" I mean that I am attempting to re-create, from a brief page of written instructions, a work of conceptual art. The instructions, written by LeWitt in 1980 and first drawn by Jo Watanabe at Larry Gagosian's gallery in Venice that same year, read like a Zen koan or a secret code comprising equal parts precision and mystery. Yet we are only the most recent people to follow these instructions—over the past twenty years or so, #343 and variations of it have been installed at galleries from Rome to Los Angeles. Some variants have the drawing as being black on white, or colored shapes on a white background.

The exact instructions, in their entirety, are as follows:

343. On a black wall, nine geometric figures (including right triangle, cross, X) in squares. The backgrounds are filled in solid white.

At the moment, we're using water-soluble crayon pastels that have the consistency of frozen butter; if held in the hand long enough, they will indeed begin to melt. We are supposed to scribble in random directions until our hands hurt and the layers of lines look almost opaque. If our hands don't hurt, according to one of LeWitt's most senior assistants, we're not doing a good job.

My hands hurt. Especially my right hand. It alternates between numbness and soreness. So I guess I'm doing a good job. We are told that the drawing should start looking right after two weeks—two weeks—of scribbling in all directions, layers upon layers of scribbles. After a while I notice that the older crayon layers are beginning to physically change, becoming more solid and brittle, in some cases flaking off when we draw over them. What started as a series of vague written instructions begins, over time, to take on a tactile, and evolving, physical presence.

Visitors constantly interrupt us as we work. Giving tours to groups during the installation of shows is part of what makes MASS MoCA unique among American art museums. It considers the installation process as valuable, and as worthy of observation, as the finished installation—it is part of its postmodern worldview. We, Julia and I, are, in effect, an interactive part of the installation. (Among the visitors who come by: artists Julie Mehretu; Simon Starling; Jenny Holzer; Chuck Close; Tara Donovan; Ed Burtynsky; Sonic Youth guitarist Lee Ranaldo and his wife, artist Leah Singer; composer Terry Riley; many school and donor groups; and Leonard Nimoy.)

When a visitor asks us what we're doing, I explain how, despite our adherence to written-out, formulaic instructions, LeWitt's wall drawings are "performed" as much as they are drawn to his specifications.

I also tell them what Anthony, LeWitt's draftsman of almost thirty years, told me with respect to #343: "Remember to draw, not color in." With #343, the drawing begins as a kind of random scribble, which is then gradually built up until it is the texture of compressed cottage cheese, if you can imagine that.

But often it's not enough to read the instructions or even to explain them—you have to be enacting them to understand.

A Line Is Not a Line But an Idea

To fully grasp the work of Sol LeWitt, one must first accept that the lines we draw are not real. Meaning, the lines made in the service of conceptual art aren't as sacrosanct as the lines used to create, say, a single original work of representational art. In the case of a LeWitt wall drawing, there is no such thing as an original, since every work can be created and re-created over and over again, per his instructions. (Of course, the commercial side of the art world dictates that access to the instructions is limited; for this particular retrospective, works such as #343 are "on loan," which means that the owner has given MASS MoCA permission to have them executed for the show.) The line is a way of mapping out or navigating the artistic gesture; it is just an approximation of an idea that might be written, for example, as "from this place to that place." LeWitt prized the idea over the execution; still, it is my business to make sure I'm successfully conveying LeWitt's idea, which for me means obsessing over the execution. As musicians well know, there are a lot of different ways to play a note, a chord, or a song, but to make it sound good—that's where the training comes in. Similarly, when a six-foot-wide circle must be drawn—in this case, by me—there are a million ways to do it, but there is only one way that LeWitt wanted it done.

Anyone familiar with LeWitt's wall drawings can tell you they all share a certain look and feel. That's because a handful of people have worked for LeWitt for much of their adult lives; they know how he wanted a given drawing to look, based on his written instructions. Early in LeWitt's career he made the drawings himself, but as demand for them grew it became necessary for him to rely on a small group of draftsmen who could faithfully carry out his instructions, developing techniques specific to each wall drawing. Those people then trained others like myself. (I first worked for LeWitt on his retrospective at the San Francisco Museum of Modern Art (SFMOMA) in 2000. For that show I was instructed in how to paint walls, mask off drawings, cut tape the correct way, make steady lines, sharpen pencil leads, minimize errors as much as humanly possible, and do extraordinarily repetitive tasks without messing things up too much.)

For example, I know that when we mask off shapes we must use a single piece of tape that can sometimes be as long as sixty feet; likewise, we must sometimes use very long lengths of paper so that when the paint is dry or the scribbling is done and the paper or tape is removed, a perfectly straight line is revealed. We are also instructed on the proper way to scribble—always in large, random strokes, never little intense strokes. Little intense strokes make an area too dark and too dense too fast.

When in doubt, I ask Anthony to check our work. The result we're going for is this: when you stand back from the drawing it's supposed to look almost solid but with all sorts of very discernible wispy lines running underneath it.

Wall Drawing #289

After completing my work on #343, I start on a crayon drawing dating back to 1977 (titled #289) that LeWitt referred to as Star Wars.

The instructions read, "Lines From Four Corners, Four Sides and the Center of a Wall to Points on a Grid."

We begin with a long rectangular black wall on which a pencil grid must be drawn (1,008 six-inch squares, to be exact). Then long white crayon lines must originate from the corners, midpoints, and center of the wall to places on the grid. The lines have to be almost perfect—but not too perfect. The lines can't be too grainy or too straight. They also can't make patterns (like a star or railroad tracks). But, strangely, the biggest dilemma we face is whether or not the edges of the wall should be considered the boundary lines of the grid—a fine distinction, to be sure, but an important one, since these drawings will become archetypal examples for future installations of LeWitt's work.

Mio is in charge of this drawing, and I'm assisting her, along with an apprentice named Jordan. A slight panic arises when Mio comes across a photograph of an earlier version of the drawing in which a crayon line touched the edge of the wall. She's unsure whether it was correct to do that or not, so she consults the principal LeWitt people—Jo Watanabe, Sachi Cho, John Hogan, Tomas Ramberg, Takeshi Akita, and finally Anthony, who has final say as to whether a drawing is being done correctly. The consensus seems to be that as the one in charge of the drawing, Mio has the right to decide whether the edge of the wall is part of the grid. In the end she decides it is.

Spock/Not-Spock

Not long after we finish #289 (it takes the three of us an entire month to complete), Leonard Nimoy visits the museum. He is part of a group looking at some of LeWitt's wall drawings from the 1970s, also recently completed. I don't notice him at first, but when I return from a Dumpster run my coworkers gush about how great it is to have just met Leonard Nimoy. I feel just a little ripped off. After all, it seems safe to assume that I am the only member of the Sol LeWitt crew who has read both of his autobiographical books, *I Am Not Spock* and the more reflective and postmodern *I Am Spock*.

It also occurs to me that Nimoy, like LeWitt, had a fictional self— for Nimoy it was the dispassionate and logical Spock, for LeWitt it was his somewhat impersonal and abstract geometric wall drawings. Everything he made was based on the grid or the space of the grid and was often done in a series. His work was not personality driven in the way that the works of Andy Warhol, Keith Haring, Jean-Michel Basquiat, Matthew Barney, or Julian Schnabel are. LeWitt, like Nimoy, is an unknown person buried deep within an abstraction.

Our paths, Nimoy's and mine, cross once again, at lunch. He glances at me as he's going out the door. He seems to be considering whether or not to smile at me, but then he decides not to.

Occasionally Emotional Geometries

Most of LeWitt's wall drawings have numbered titles bestowed in the order of their making. Despite the emphasis on numbers and geometry, LeWitt's line drawings, because of the number of people required to realize them, are as humanly complex as they are (seemingly) mechanically simplistic. By having so many people put so much energy into the pieces, a certain psychological intensity can be discerned from close examination. If his wall drawings create an intense phenomenological experience, it's because their scale is a by-product of his logical approach and his insistence on making variations of his works—not because of any preoccupation with trying to make work that is phenomenological on its own.

So it should come as no surprise that his wall drawings of shapes and lines aren't inherently emotional or sentimental. That is, except for a work from 1970 known as:

#46. Vertical lines, not straight, not touching, covering the wall evenly.

This drawing gives the impression of long streaming hair, of waves on the sea, or of a river flowing past. It conveys a sense of loss. This work was supposedly for or inspired by the artist Eva Hesse, who died of a brain tumor in 1970, at the age of thirty-four. The first installation of this drawing was done in Paris the year Hesse died, and LeWitt himself was the one who installed it.

#46 also recalls a woodblock print by Edvard Munch, which *is* sentimental. It's called simply *Man's Head in Woman's Hair.*

One of the few times I actually got to talk with LeWitt was at SFMOMA in 2000. It was at the party celebrating the end of the installation of his first retrospective there, which I had worked on as well. While he was pouring champagne for people, I asked him about #46. I remember he was a little vague but acknowledged its association with Hesse, whom he'd known in New York in the 1960s.

Later at the party I remember asking him if he would pose for a picture with me and a cube I'd made of paper (a symbol of human logic). He smiled, amused, and told me he'd made a lot of paper cubes in his time but that now other people made them for him.

The Geographically Apt Thoreau Connection

On April 8, approximately a week after we'd begun work on the MASS MoCA installation, our team assembled near several enormous blank walls for a moment of silence. It had been exactly one year since LeWitt had died. Anthony said that LeWitt wouldn't have wanted us to make much fuss about the anniversary. Nonetheless it was his work that had brought all of us together, and it seemed important to acknowledge his absence. In life he had always been very generous and frequently gave his art to his friends and his assistants. He also employed many people over the years and helped other artists with their careers.

When the retrospective opens in November 2008 it will be an art show as much as it is a tribute to the tension between the individual and society—a tribute located, not so coincidentally, in the same state where Henry David Thoreau's cabin still sits on Walden Pond. LeWitt's is art that Thoreau perhaps would have enjoyed. Thoreau, who strove to simplify his life to its bare, essential elements, might have seen LeWitt's instruction-based drawings as on par with his handmade cabin, chairs, and tables.

In *Walden*, he wrote, "I had three chairs in my house; one for solitude, two for friendship, three for society."

Return to Hayneville

Gregory Orr

"When I write prose," says Gregory Orr, "I find myself acknowledging truths that elude me in poetry—how one event follows another; how our actions and choices become our destinies; how randomness and chance preside over much of what happens. I also see how much larger than a single self the world is. When I write poetry, the self, the "I," has to be at the center because a single consciousness is what constellates the language in a lyric. But when I write prose, especially a prose piece like this one, which is so entangled in history and its forces, I see how small an individual self really is." In this essay, which appeared in the Virginia Quarterly Review, *Orr recalls his own small role in the civil rights movement.*

I was born and raised in rural, upstate New York, but who I am began with a younger brother's death in a hunting accident when I was twelve and he was eight. I held the gun that killed him. But if my life began at twelve with my brother's sudden, violent death, then my end, determined by the trajectory of that harsh beginning, could easily have taken place a scant six years later, when, in June 1965, I was kidnapped at gunpoint by vigilantes near the small town of Hayneville, Alabama.

When I was sixteen, in my senior year of high school, I became involved in the civil rights movement partly because I hoped I could lose myself in that worthwhile work. I became a member of CORE (Congress of Racial Equality) and canvassed door-to-door in poorer neighborhoods in the nearby city of Kingston. I traveled down to Atlantic City with a carload of CORE members to picket the Democratic National Convention in August 1964. Earlier that summer, the Mississippi Freedom Democratic Party—another civil rights group—had chosen a slate of racially integrated delegates to challenge Mississippi's all-white official Democratic Party delegates for seats at the convention. The goal was to put Lyndon Johnson and the whole liberal wing of the party on the spot—testing their commitment to change. I was one of about twenty or so people parading in a small circle on the dilapidated boardwalk outside the convention hall. We carried signs urging on the drama inside: SUPPORT THE FREEDOM DELEGATION and ONE MAN, ONE VOTE. I felt confused and thrilled and purposeful all at the same time.

Three marchers carried poles, each bearing a huge charcoal portrait of a different young man. Their larger-than-life faces gazed down at us as we walked our repetitious circle. They were renditions of Andrew Goodman, James Chaney, and Michael Schwerner, SNCC (Student Nonviolent Coordinating Committee) volunteers who had been missing for months, whose bodies had only recently been discovered. They had last been seen alive on June 21, driving away from the Neshoba County sheriff's office in Philadelphia, Mississippi. When an informer led investigators to the spot where their tortured bodies had been bulldozed into a clay dam, the mystery of their whereabouts ended abruptly and they began a second life—the life of martyrs to a cause. Those three faces mesmerized us as we circled the boardwalk, singing and trying to ignore the heckling from bystanders. The artist who had drawn them had resolved their faces into a few bold lines that gave them a subtle dignity. They seemed at peace, all their uncertainties and inner complexities over. I longed to be like them, to transcend my confusions and the agonies of my past and be taken up into some noble simplicity beyond change. I longed to sacrifice myself and escape myself—to become a martyr for the movement. If it took death to gain access to the grandeur of meaning, so be it. And thus are young soldiers born.

I was too young, only seventeen, to go to Mississippi that summer, but a year later I was on my way. I drove south, alone, in a '56 Ford my father had bought me for the trip. And so it commenced—my instruction in the grim distance between the myth of the martyr and the intimate reality of violence.

CUT TO NOVEMBER 2006—over forty years have passed since my late-adolescent misadventures in the Deep South. I'm a poet and a professor—that's how I've spent my life. One of the happier perquisites of my profession is that I'm sometimes asked to read my poems at various colleges and universities. One such invitation has come my way—a former student of mine, a poet named Chris, is teaching at Auburn University and has invited me down. I'm reading that same week in Atlanta, and as I look over my Rand McNally, I see that I can not only drive from Atlanta to Auburn, I can proceed an hour or so farther and drive straight through time and into my own past. I decide to go back to Hayneville—the tiny town that has been so long lodged like a sliver in my memory.

Chris says he'll take the trip with me, and he brings Brian, a former student of his own. I'm glad of the company. Three poets from three generations: I'll turn sixty within the year, Chris is in his early forties,

Brian in his midtwenties. As we leave town in my rented, economy-
size Hyundai, pulling onto the interstate in the late-afternoon drizzle,
Brian asks where we're headed. For several days, I've felt a quiet tension about this trip, and suddenly it seems I can release some of the
tension by telling Brian and Chris the story of that long-ago summer.
At first, I try to talk about what happened to me in Hayneville itself,
but I quickly see that I'll have to start further back in order to make a
coherent story of it.

As we drive down the highway toward Montgomery, I feel like one
of those pilgrims in Chaucer, challenged by my travel companions to
entertain them on the journey. Brian's in the backseat, and as I begin
my story, I occasionally turn my head slightly as if acknowledging
I'm aware of him as an audience, but soon I'll become so caught up
in the narrative that I'll lose all sense of my companions and of time
and distance passing. I'll drive steadily toward Hayneville, as though
the story and the highway were a single, fused flowing.

It was late May 1965. After brief training, another volunteer, a
man from Pittsburgh named Steve, and I were assigned to work in
Bolivar County, Mississippi—the Delta region, where COFO (Council of Federated Organizations) was trying to gain momentum for a
strike of field workers. The going wage was $4 a day—dawn to dusk
hoeing the cotton by hand, everyone from seven-year-old kids to
octogenarians. We'd been in Bolivar only a week or so, helping out at
the office. Suddenly, there was a summons from headquarters: everyone who could be mustered and spared from their local work—any
new volunteers and all the local residents who could be persuaded—
should report to the state capital in Jackson. The governor of Mississippi had called a secret session of the legislature, and the movement
was organizing a mass demonstration to draw national attention to
what it suspected was serious political skulduggery.

At ten in the morning on June 14, about five hundred of us—men, women, teenagers, old folks—assembled in Jackson. We walked two abreast down the sidewalk toward the capitol building. Our leaders told us we'd be stopped by the police and warned we could not parade without a permit. At that point, we would have to choose to be arrested or to disperse. We were urged to let ourselves be arrested—the plan was to fill the jail to overflowing and apply the steady pressure of media and economics (they'll have to feed and house us at city expense). The powers-that-be had learned to present a sanitized image to the media, so our arrest was very polite—journalists and photographers there watched each of us ushered onto a truck by two city policemen who held us by both arms, firmly but calmly. The trucks themselves were large, enclosed vehicles—the kind you'd use to transport chairs for a rally or municipal lawnmowers. They packed about thirty of us inside, then closed the doors. And we were off—each truck with its own motorcycle escort gliding through red lights, heading, we presumed, toward the city jail. But the actual destination was our first big surprise. We activists may have had a plan to demonstrate, but the State of Mississippi and the City of Jackson had their own plan. We were taken to the county fairgrounds—twenty or so fenced acres of clear-cut land set with half a dozen long, low, tin-roofed barns. Another thing we didn't know: when each truck entered the fairgrounds, the gate swung shut behind it, and police turned back anyone else who tried to enter.

The truck I was on stopped, backed up, then came to a final halt. When the doors opened and our eyes adjusted to the flood of light, we saw we weren't at the jail at all—but in a narrow alley between two barns. A score of uniformed officers was gathered there, wearing the uniforms of motorcycle cops—tall leather boots, mirrored sunglasses, and blue helmets with the black earflaps pulled down. Each tanned face was almost indistinguishable under its partial disguise—only the nose and mouth showing—some already grinning at the joke of our surprise and what was in store for us. Each of them had his nightstick out—some tapping their clubs rhythmically in the palms of their hands, others just standing there expectantly with the stick held at each end. I didn't notice until I was up close and even then, in my confusion, didn't comprehend that the lower half of each officer's silver badge, where the identifying number should have been displayed, was neatly covered with black tape. An officer ordered us to climb down, and when some of us didn't, two officers climbed up and pushed us to the edge, where others pulled us down. And it began. They swung their clubs right and left, randomly but thoroughly, for about ten minutes. It made no difference what you did, whether you screamed or were silent—you were struck again and again and, if you fell to the ground, kicked. It hurts—to be beaten over the head or back or shoulders with a wooden club. It's also terrifying. Then an order came and the clubbing stopped—we were told to get up (one kid couldn't and was dragged away somewhere, his leg too damaged to stand on).

We filed through a door into one of the barns. Inside, there was a calm that felt surreal after the violence outside. In the middle of the empty concrete floor, five card tables had been set up in a row, each with a typewriter and a city policeman seated in a folding chair. The far end of the barn, half hidden in shadow, was a milling cluster of frightened women and girls who, their initial beating and processing over, had been told to assemble there. Our dazed group lined up, and each of us in turn was formally processed and charged. The women from our truck were sent to join the other women at the far end of the barn. I was told to go out one of the side doors to the next barn where the men were being confined. Just as I was about to go through the door, an officer told me to take my straw hat off and carry it in my hands. I emerged into the outdoors and the bright sunlight and saw them—two lines of about fifteen highway patrolmen on either side. I was ordered to walk, not run, between them. Again, I was beaten with nightsticks, but this time more thoroughly as I was the only target. When I covered my head with raised arms to ward off the first blow from the officer on my right, I was jabbed in the ribs with a club from the other side. Instinctively, I pivoted in that direction, only to be left vulnerable in the other. I heard blows and felt sharp pokes or slaps fall flat and hard across my ribs and back from both directions—whether they were simultaneous or alternating, it made no difference; my defense was hopeless. By the time I neared the end of this gantlet, I was cringing from feinted blows—the humiliation of my fear and their laughter far worse than the physical pain.

Inside the other barn, men and boys were assembled in a dense clump surrounded by a loose ring of officers. Later that afternoon we would go through another ritually structured set of beatings. When anyone tried to sit down or move out to the edge of the impacted group to get some air, two or three officers dashed across the small, intervening space and beat him with clubs. This technique was designed to make us prisoners panic and fight one another to get to the safer center of the mass. But it didn't work. We tried to protect ourselves as best we could and keep the most vulnerable, especially the children, safe in the middle. A bearded young man in our group was noticeably defiant, and at a certain point an officer ran in and deftly struck him with a slicing motion of the blunt end of his nightstick in such a way that the taut skin of his forehead split and blood streamed down over the whole of his face. To see an individual human face suddenly turned into a mask of blood is to witness the eradication of the personal, and, if you're standing nearby as I was, to be sickened and unnerved.

The hours went by as more prisoners were processed and our group continued to grow—there were over a hundred and fifty men and boys in the barn. Evening fell. We were ordered to sit in rows on the concrete floor—three feet apart, three feet between the rows. We didn't know it, but we were waiting for mattresses to be delivered.

We were told to sit bolt upright and not move; officers walked up and down the rows. If you leaned a hand down to rest or shifted your weight, a shouting patrolman rushed up with his club raised.

A black kid of maybe ten or twelve sat next to me. We'd been there for an hour and things were pretty quiet when a state patrolman stopped in front of the boy. He looked him over for a minute, then ordered him to take off the pin he was wearing—one of those movement buttons that said FREEDOM NOW or ONE MAN, ONE VOTE. No safety clasp, just an open pin. The guard told the kid to pull the pin off his shirt. He did. "Put it in your mouth," the guard said. I turned my head to the right and saw the boy place it in his mouth. "Swallow it," the guard said, his voice menacing, but not loud. If the kid tried to swallow it, the pin would choke him or pierce his throat and lodge there until he bled to death in agony.

Watching the scene, I felt murderous rage fill my whole being, geysering up in the single second it took to see what seemed about to happen. I became nothing but the impulse to scramble to my feet, grab the guard's pistol before he knew what was happening, and shoot him as many times as possible. Nothing but that intense impulse and a very small voice inside me that said: "You don't stand a chance. It would take longer than you imagine—long enough for him to turn on you, for his buddies to rush up and grab you. And then what? You would be their sudden and absolute target."

How long did that moment last? How long did the guard loom over the boy with his threats? How long did the boy sit there with the pin in his mouth, tasting its metallic bitterness but refusing to swallow, or unable to swallow? It could have been five minutes; it could have been less. The guard repeated his command several times, along with profanities. And then, other officers were there, urging him to give it up, persuading him to move on, to move away.

The mattresses finally arrived, and each of us dragged one off to his place in a row. We were officially segregated according to the laws of the sovereign state of Mississippi—a vigilantly patrolled lane separated two imaginary cell blocks, one for blacks and one for whites. We lay down to sleep. The pounding of nightsticks on the concrete floor woke us at dawn, and we realized the highway patrolmen who had abused us with such relish and impunity the previous day were nowhere in sight. They'd been replaced by Fish and Game wardens who looked altogether more rustic and thoughtful (some even had moustaches) and made no effort to conceal their badge numbers and even wore name tags. Later that morning, a plainclothes officer entered our barn and announced that the FBI had arrived and that if anyone had complaints about their treatment, they should step forward to be interviewed. I did so and was ushered out into the same alley where we'd first been greeted and beaten. The narrow lane had been rigged at one end with an awning for shade. Under the awning, four FBI agents sat at small desks. When my turn came, I told my narrative about the beatings, but how could I identify the perpetrators? The agent asked if I could specify hair or eye color, or badge number? I couldn't. Could I point out now, in person, any of the officers who had beaten me? They weren't there, of course—they'd left in the middle of the night. The agent recorded my story of the previous day's beatings and violence and thanked me for my time. If they had actually wanted to protect us, the FBI could easily have arrived anytime the preceding day. Many in the movement already knew what was inconceivable to me at the time—that events like this were stage-managed and that the FBI wasn't a friend or even a neutral ally of the civil rights movement.

For the next ten days, we lay each morning on our mattresses until breakfast—grits and a molasses syrup and powdered milk so watered down I could see all the way to the bottom of the fifty-gallon pot that held it. After breakfast, we rolled up our mattresses and either sat all day on the concrete floor or paced the imaginary confines of our collective cell. Twice a day, we were lined up for the bathroom—it was then or never as we stood pressed up against one another, waiting for our brief turn in one of the five stinking stalls. No showers, no chance to wash at all, the same, reeking clothes day after day. Hot as hell once the sun heated the tin roof, but chill at night when we huddled, blanketless, in the dark on our bare mattresses. The mosquito fogger sprayed around the outside of the barn each evening, sending its toxic cloud in under the closed doors to set us all coughing. Boredom, stench, heat. Word came from outside—we could, at any time, be released by posting a $50 bond that the movement would provide, but the plan called for as many as possible to stay inside for as long as we could. There was hope we would seriously inconvenience the state by staying, that another demonstration in support of us might take place—there was even talk of Martin Luther King Jr. himself showing up for it. Rumors and hope; and a request to persevere. Most of us stayed, though some of the youngest and oldest chose to leave. The violence mostly gone; if it occurred, it was sporadic and spontaneous and ended quickly without major consequence. Exhausted by lack of substantial food, worn down by boredom and discomfort, I gradually lost heart. I had dreamed of meaningful work and even heroic martyrdom, but here I was merely cannon fodder. I held a place; I counted—but only as an integer in the calculus of a complex political game playing out in rooms far above me. And close up, as close as the arc of a swung billy club, I had discovered that for every martyr whose life was resolved into a meaningful death, there were hundreds of others who were merely beaten, terrorized, humiliated. Even as I sank into depression and brooded in the stifling heat of that jail-barn, I was learning that I wanted to live.

On the tenth day there, my name was called and I was led outside and taken to a pay phone attached to a post near our barn. Picking up the receiver, I heard the voice of my father's lawyer, who was calling from upstate New York. We'd only met once; I hardly knew him. He began by saying he couldn't stand me or any of the causes I believed in, but my father was his dear friend and was frantic with worry. My fine had been paid. I was to leave now and drive back north immediately if I cared a damn about my family. End of story. His tongue-lashing eliminated the last of my resolve. The officer standing beside me took me in a patrol car to where I'd left the Ford ten days ago, as if the whole thing had been prearranged.

I should have called the COFO office and told them I was leaving, was heading north that very day—but I was ashamed. I was deserting—a frightened and confused teenager. The map told me my quickest route north was by state roads from Jackson to Selma, Alabama, and then on to Montgomery, where the interstate began. When I passed through Selma it was early evening and I was starved (we'd been fed nothing but vegetables and grits for ten days), but I was too afraid to stop for dinner.

It was dusk on US 80, past Selma and within fifteen miles of Montgomery, when I heard a siren. A white car pulled up close behind me, flashing its lights. I thought it was a police car and pulled over, but the two men who jumped out, one tall and rather thin, the other shorter and stout, wore no uniforms. They did each wear holsters, and as they approached, one on each side of my car, they drew their pistols. I rolled up my windows and locked my doors. Rap of a pistol barrel on the window two inches from my head: "Get out, you son of a bitch, or I'll blow your head off."

I got out and stood on the road's shoulder, beside my car. They prodded me with their guns and told me they were going to kill me. They searched my car and found SNCC pamphlets in the trunk. They were sure I was an agitator rumored to be coming to their town— my New York license plates had been a strong clue that the pamphlets confirmed. The men made two promises about my immediate future. The first was that they would kill me and dump my body in the swamps. The second, made a few moments later, was that they were going to take me to a jail, where I would rot. With those two contradictory threats left floating in the air, they took my wallet and went back to their vehicle, ordering me to follow them in my own car. They pulled onto the highway and zoomed off. I started my car and followed them. We hadn't driven more than a mile when they signaled and turned off to the right, onto a smaller road. I hesitated, uncertain what to do, then made the turn and followed.

I PAUSE IN this story I'm telling Chris and Brian when I realize we've reached the green sign marking the turnoff for Hayneville. I'd been so caught up in telling it that I hardly noticed we'd passed through Montgomery and were speeding down Route 80 toward Selma. Suddenly, I realize the old story and my present journey are eerily coinciding at this forlorn intersection. It's as if my ghost Ford from forty years ago is approaching the turnoff from the west, coming from Selma, at the same moment that my shiny white rental reaches that same turn from the direction of Montgomery. The terrified boy in the ghost Ford drives right into us, and for a moment, we and the story are one and the same. Now, I'm driving slowly down that back road toward Hayneville, telling Chris and Brian what it felt like the first time I took this road, alone, following the car driven by my would-be killers.

Their car was newer than mine and faster. It sped up. A voice in my head started screaming: "What are you doing? You are obligingly speeding to your own death—driving to your own grave! Turn around and make a run for it!" But how could I? They had my wallet with my license and all my money. It was pitch-dark now. The road was so narrow there was no place to turn around; there were swamps on either side. If I tried to make a getaway, their car could easily overtake mine, and they would surely shoot me. This hysterical dialogue raged in my head for the ten long minutes of that ride, and then we emerged out of the dark into Hayneville. We passed the courthouse, pulled into a narrow street, and stopped in back of a small jail.

Even as I describe that terrifying drive, I see that the wooded swamps are gone. (Or were they imagined in the dark so long ago?) It's mostly fields and pasture with a pond here and there gleaming like oil in the deepening gloom. And now we're arriving in the town itself. Again, as with the first time I was here, it's almost completely dark under the overarching trees, only a glimpse of a gray sky from which all trace of light is gone. I recognize things: there is the courthouse— no wonder it stood out—white and two stories high on its tree-filled lawn in a town of twenty or so tiny houses and bungalows. And there is something completely new in town (the only new thing as far as I can see)—a BP convenience store, where I stop for gas. The station is shiny and all lit up, its blue-green signs glowing intensely in the dark like those roadside stores in Edward Hopper paintings, gleaming forlornly against the primeval dark of rural Anywhere, America. I'm trembling with a kind of giddy excitement as I pump the gas. Even here I can see changes—the man behind the counter in the station, whom I take to be the owner, is black; so are most of his customers. Back then, whites owned everything. As I pull my car out of the station across from the courthouse, I see that the sheriff's car, just now parking beside the small police bungalow behind the courthouse, is driven by a black officer.

WHEN WE GOT to the jail forty years ago, I felt relieved. At least the terrifying drive was over. But my torment was only entering another phase. I'd be held there in solitary confinement without charges for eight days. I was kept on the second floor the entire time, separate from all other prisoners and personnel, seeing and talking to no one except the silent trustee who brought me food twice a day and took away my empty tray. Why was I so isolated from the rest of the prisoners? It was possible they didn't want people to know where I was as they waited to find out if anyone was aware that I was "missing." Ever since the murders of Goodman, Schwerner, and Chaney, volunteers were under strict orders to check in with headquarters before traveling any distance, to record their destination and expected arrival time, so that if anything went wrong an alert could be sent out for an immediate search. I hadn't called, so no one knew I was in Hayneville's jail.

Four days into my incarceration, my father's lawyer called the DA in Jackson, Mississippi, to ask if he knew why I hadn't arrived home. The DA didn't know; they'd let me go. Then he tried the state attorney general's office in Montgomery, which was run at the time by Richmond Flowers, a racial moderate. His office made inquiries and learned I was being held in Hayneville, but they couldn't offer any help. They told Dad's lawyer that Lowndes County resisted all outside interference, even from Alabama state authorities. On my fifth day there, my father's lawyer managed to call the jail and was told (by the sheriff himself, slyly posing as a deputy) that indeed a young man named Greg Orr was there and was at that moment playing checkers with the sheriff.

Of course this was a lie. I had no knowledge of the call, no sense that anyone in the world knew where I was. Each day I spent in that cell was an eternity. I was unmoored from structures except food and the alternation of day and night. I didn't know when my spell in solitary would end. If someone had said to me: "You'll be kept alone in a small cell with no one to speak to for eight days," I could have tried to organize the ordeal in my mind—I could have, for starters, kept track of the days and known that each one passing brought me closer to the end. But there was no known end point and so no measurement—it was wholly arbitrary and made me even more aware of my own powerlessness. Already depressed and disoriented by the ten days in "jail" in Jackson, I was even more frightened in Hayneville: I had a better sense of how dangerous my situation was, and my imagination took over from there.

In the middle of my eighth day the sheriff came to my cell, unlocked it, and told me I was free to go. That was it: no apology, no formal charges, no anything. I was taken to my car, told to get out of town. I was set free as abruptly and mysteriously as I had been captured and incarcerated. I got in my car and drove. I drove and drove. I have one memory of stopping in some rest area in South Carolina in the middle of the night and trying to wash and shave, but my hands were shaking too much to control the razor. I slept whenever I couldn't drive any longer, pulling into parking lots and climbing into the backseat. By the time I reached New Jersey, I was hallucinating huge rats running across the highway in front of my headlights. And then I was home, back in the Hudson River Valley town I'd left only a month or so earlier.

I spent July in my hometown, but in early August I took a job in New York with a small film company, synchronizing sound and picture. On my way home from work one August day, I bought a *New York Times* to read on the subway. When I looked at the front page, I saw a story about a murder that had just taken place in Hayneville. I turned to the inner page to finish the article and was stunned to see a photograph of one of the men who had kidnapped me on the highway. The news article related that he had shotgunned Jonathan Daniels, an Episcopalian seminary student and civil rights volunteer, in broad daylight on the courthouse lawn, in front of half a dozen witnesses. From what I could tell, the victim and the others with him might have been the "outside agitators" whom I had been mistaken for. According to the newspaper, they, like me, had been arbitrarily arrested and held without charges for days in the jail and then suddenly released. But unlike me, they had no car. They spent several hours desperately trying to find someone to drive them to Montgomery, while the murderer, a friend of the sheriff's and a "special unpaid deputy," became more and more agitated. He found the released organizers near the courthouse and aimed his shotgun at a young black woman, Ruby Sales. The seminary student pushed her aside and stood in front just as the gun went off.

Though the man was charged with murder, the verdict, given by a local all-white jury in that very courthouse, was "not guilty" on the basis of self-defense. The same courthouse later saw the trial of the killers of Viola Liuzzo, the Detroit housewife who, three months before my arrival in town, had participated in the Selma to Montgomery march. On the evening of March 25, she was killed by gunfire while ferrying marchers in her car on Route 80. Her slayers, quickly apprehended, were also found not guilty by another all-white Hayneville jury, even though eyewitness prosecution testimony was given by one of the four Klansmen (a paid FBI informer) present that night in the murder car.

My situation in Hayneville resembled the seminary student's: arbitrary arrest, jail time without arraignment or trial, and then sudden release. But I had a car, and timing mattered: the *New York Times* article stressed that the killer had been upset about the passage of the Voting Rights Act—as if part of his motivation was a kind of crazed act of political protest. When I was apprehended and jailed, the status quo in Hayneville seemed secure—if my presence there was a sign of change, it was the sort of change they felt they could easily contain and control.

Two others died there—a murder in March; another in August— and in between, in late June, my own narrow escape as I slipped through the same violent landscape. "Slipped through" makes me sound like a fish that found a hole in the net, but surely I was trapped in it, surely it was luck that pulled me from its entanglements and casually tossed me back into the sea.

———

AND HERE I am again, forty-one years later, approaching the jail, that brick edifice in which all my emotions and memories of Hayneville are concentrated. Not the memory or idea of jail, but this dingy incarnation of incarceration—a building full of little cages where people are captive. I've been monologuing until now, spewing out non-stop the whole story that brought me here, but as we travel the last few blocks, I go silent with anticipation. Chris and Brian are also quiet but excited. Now that we're in the town itself, certain key nouns connect to real things—there is the courthouse pretty much as I described it. And here, down this little lane a half block past the courthouse, is the jail itself, that brick, L-shaped building I've been talking about. But how different it is from what I remembered and described! It's an empty husk. Boarded up—from the looks of it, abandoned a number of years ago. Deserted, dilapidated, the mortar rotted out between the grimy bricks. The only thing not in utter disrepair is a small exercise yard attached to the back, behind a chain-link fence topped with razor wire.

When I stop in the cinder parking lot and hop out of the car, I feel like a kid who has arrived at a playground. I'm surprised by my responses. Here, at a place that was a locus of some of the most intense misery I've ever known, I'm feeling curiously happy. Chris and Brian have also climbed out. I can see they're glad, too—pleased to have found some real, palpable thing at the end of a tunnel of words burrowing from the distant past. Chris has a camera and begins to take pictures, though it's night now and there's no way of knowing if anything will register. The doors to the building are locked, but Brian, exploring the fence's gate, finds it's open, and we're able to enter the yard. We climb some rusty steps to a second-floor landing; from there I can point to the window that was across the corridor from my cell and that I peered out of after shinnying up my cell door's bars and craning my neck. That giddiness I felt when I first set my feet on the parking lot has been growing more intense—I'm laughing now, and when I'm not laughing, I'm unable to stop grinning. Earlier, in the car, telling the stories of my long-ago misadventures, the words had zipped directly from my brain's private memory to my tongue in a kind of nonstop narrative that mostly bypassed my emotions. Now my brain has stopped functioning almost entirely, and I'm taken over by this odd laughter that's bubbling up from some wordless source far down in my body—some deep, cellular place.

Brian and Chris poke around the weed-grown yard, looking for anything interesting, some rusty artifact to point to or pick up and ponder. I'm ordinarily a person who likes souvenirs—a shell from a beach, a rock from a memorable walk in the woods—but I have no wish to take anything physical from this place. Even a pebble would weigh me down, and the truth is I feel weightless right now, as if I'm a happy spirit moving through a scene of desolation.

MY BEGINNING WAS a rifle shot and someone innocent suddenly dead. My end might well have been something eerily similar: perhaps a pistol shot, my own death in this tiny town so far from my home—a beginning and end so close to each other as to render the life cryptic and tragic by way of its brevity. Only, Hayneville *wasn't* my end. It was a place where my life could have ended but didn't, and now, almost half a century later, I stand beside that closed-down, dilapidated jail, laughing. But laughing at what, at whom? Not at the confused and earnest kid I was all those years ago, the one who blundered through and escaped thanks to blind luck. What is this laughter that's fountaining up through me?

As we're leaving and I pause in the cindery parking lot with one hand on my car-door handle, taking a last look at the old jail, a single word comes to me: *joy*. It's joy I'm feeling—joy is at the heart of this peculiar laughter. Joy is my body's primal response to the enormity of the gift it has been given—a whole life! A whole life was there waiting for me the day I left this town. A life full of joys I couldn't imagine back then: a long, deeply satisfying marriage to a woman I love, two wonderful daughters, forty years of writing poems and teaching the craft of poetry. Laughing to think that the kid I was had come south seeking the dark blessing of death in a noble cause, but had instead been given the far more complex blessing of life, given his whole existence and all the future struggle to sort it out and make it significant—to himself and, if he was lucky as a writer, to others also. Laughing at how my life went on past this town and blossomed into its possibilities, one of which (shining in the dark) was love.

about the contributors

Amy Andrews has worked as a high school English teacher for the past ten years. She earned her MFA in Creative Writing from the Rainier Writing Workshop at Pacific Lutheran University. Her work has appeared in the *Gettysburg Review*. She lives in the middle of a nature park in Rochester, New York, with her husband, two children, and an assortment of animals.

Stan Badgett and his wife live in the mountains of western Colorado, where they raised four children. Badgett currently teaches English at Alpine Christian Academy and Colorado Mountain College. His work has appeared in literary journals including *Fulcrum* and *Dirty Goat*. He is writing a memoir about growing up in the West and working in the coal mines.

Julianna Baggott is the author of fifteen books: six novels, including *The Madam*; three collections of poetry, most recently *Lizzie Borden in Love*; and six novels for younger readers, most notably *The Prince of Fenway Park* and *The Anybodies* trilogy, under the pen name N. E. Bode. She teaches in the creative writing program at Florida State University. Her work has appeared in the *New York Times*, *Real Simple*, and *Best American Poetry*, and has been read on NPR's "Talk of the Nation."

Tim Bascom's memoir *Chameleon Days* (Houghton Mifflin, 2006) won the Bakeless Literary Prize in Nonfiction and was a finalist for the PEN USA

Literary Award. His essays have won editor's prizes from the *Missouri Review* and the *Florida Review* and have appeared in a wide range of journals and in anthologies such as *Best American Travel Writing*. Bascom is also the author of the novel *Squatters' Rites* and a collection of essays titled *The Comfort Trap*. He is a graduate of the Nonfiction Writing Program at the University of Iowa and currently lives in Des Moines, Iowa.

Scott Black has had the good fortune to attend Northland College, University of Baltimore, Auburn University, and Ohio State's Creative Writing Program. He currently lives in Columbus, Ohio, and would like to get out in the woods more often.

Laura Bramon Good lives with her husband, Ben, in Washington, DC, where she works on human trafficking issues. She holds an MA from the Johns Hopkins University Writing Seminar.

Chris Cobb is an artist based in San Francisco who sometimes writes. His work has been in *Flash Art, ArtWeek, TENbyTEN,* and McSweeney's online and has been exhibited at Adobe Bookshop in San Francisco, ATM Gallery in New York, and Gallery Onetwentyeight in New York, among others. He is represented by the Eleanor Harwood Gallery in San Francisco.

Margaret Conway has an MFA from San Francisco State, where she has taught creative writing. She lives in San Francisco. "Grasshopper" is a reworked segment of text from an unpublished memoir, *Night Light: Story of an Arson*, that recounts the aftermath of a night when the author and her husband awoke to find their place in flames. The chapter titled "Grasshopper" is the part that didn't fit, the part that seemed to need a place of its own.

Michael Copperman has an MFA in fiction writing from the University of Oregon, where he currently teaches writing to at-risk students of color. His nonfiction has appeared in *Brevity*, the *Oregonian*, the *Register-Guard*, and the *Eugene Weekly*; his fiction has appeared in *Thirdreader* and the *Arkansas Review*. From 2002 to 2004 he taught fourth grade in the rural black public schools of the Mississippi Delta, and he is working on a book about that experience. He blogs at Spade's a Spade, or The Burden of Being Right.

Edwidge Danticat was born in Haiti and moved to the United States when she was twelve. She is the author of several books, including *Breath, Eyes, Memory*, an Oprah Book Club selection; *Krik? Krak!* a National Book Award finalist; *The Farming of Bones*, an American Book Award winner; and the novel-in-stories, *The Dew Breaker*. She is also the editor of *The Butterfly's Way: Voices from the Haitian Dyaspora in the United States* and *The Beacon Best of 2000: Great Writing by Men and Women of All Colors and Cultures* and has written two young adult novels, *Anacaona, Golden Flower* and *Behind the Mountains*, as well as a travel narrative, *After the Dance, A Walk Through Carnival in Jacmel*. Her most recent book is *Brother, I'm Dying*, a memoir.

Aislinn Doyle lives in the Dominican Republic, where she is completing a postgraduate fellowship with an educational nonprofit organization called the DREAM Project, an experience she writes about in her blog, steal your imagination. She recently received a Masters in Education from Harvard University, where she focused her studies on how the artistic process functions as a learning process. She is originally from Framingham, Massachusetts.

Alice Dreger is Clinical Professor of Medical Humanities and Bioethics in the Medical Humanities and Bioethics Program of the Feinberg School of Medicine at Northwestern University in Chicago, a Guggenheim Fellow, and a voluntary patient advocate for people born with norm-challenging bodies. Her books include *Hermaphrodites and the Medical Invention of Sex* (1998) and *One of Us: Conjoined Twins and the Future of Normal* (2004), both with Harvard University Press. Her essays on science, medicine, and life have appeared in the *New York Times*, the *Washington Post*, and the *Wall Street Journal*, and she has appeared as a talking head (and once as a dancer) on many broadcast programs, including ABC's *20/20*, NPR's *All Things Considered*, and the *Oprah Winfrey Show*. She lives with her partner-patron and their son in East Lansing, Michigan.

John Griswold is the author of a novel, *A Democracy of Ghosts*. He's also published stories, essays, and poems in *Ninth Letter*, *Brevity*, *Natural Bridge*, *Perigee*, and *War, Literature & the Arts*. As Oronte Churm, he's a columnist for McSweeney's Internet Tendency and keeps the blog The Education of Oronte Churm at InsideHigherEd.com.

Jeffrey Ethan Lee's poetry book *identity papers* (Ghost Road Press, 2006) was a 2007 Colorado Book Award finalist. He also published the poetry book *invisible sister* (Many Mountains Moving Press, 2004); *The Sylf* (2003), the 2002 winner of the Sow's Ear Poetry Chapbook prize; and *Strangers in a Homeland* (Ashland Poetry Press chapbook). He also won the first Tupelo Press award for literary fiction in 2001 for a novel, *The Autobiography of Somebody Else*. He currently teaches creative writing at West Chester University.

Jay Lewenstein lives in Mexicali, Mexico, and teaches community college English on the U.S. side of the border. Currently, he is developing an anthology of short stories that reflect the spirit and culture of border.

Brenda Miller is the author of *Season of the Body* (Sarabande Books, 2002) and coauthor of *Tell It Slant: Writing and Shaping Creative Nonfiction* (McGraw-Hill, 2003). "Table of Figures" appears in her newest collection of essays, *Blessing of the Animals* (Eastern Washington University Press, 2009). Her work has received five Pushcart Prizes. She is an associate professor of English at Western Washington University and serves as editor in chief of the *Bellingham Review*.

Marie Mutsuki Mockett was born in Carmel, California, to a Japanese mother and an American father. She is a graduate of Columbia University with a degree in East Asian studies, and her work has been published in numerous journals, including *AGNI*, *LIT*, *Epoch*, *North Dakota Quarterly*, and *Phoebe*. Her debut novel, *Picking Bones from Ash*, will be released by Graywolf Press in fall 2009. She lives with her Scottish husband in New York City.

Christina Olson's first book of poems, *Before I Came Home Naked*, is forthcoming from Spire Press. Her poetry and creative nonfiction can be found in *Puerto del Sol*, *Hayden's Ferry Review*, *Brevity*, *Black Warrior Review*, and other publications. Originally from Buffalo, New York, she is currently a visiting assistant professor of writing at Grand Valley State University in Michigan. Her blog is called dbdsn.

Gregory Orr is the author of ten collections of poetry, the most recent of which is *How Beautiful the Beloved* (Copper Canyon Press, 2009) and a memoir, *The Blessing* (Council Oak Books, 2005), which was chosen by *Publisher's Weekly* as one of the fifty best nonfiction books of 2005. He teaches at the University of Virginia, where he founded the MFA Program in Writing.

Emily Rapp is the author of *Poster Child: A Memoir* (BloomsburyUSA). Her work has appeared in *The Sun*, *StoryQuarterly*, *Narrative*, *Good House-*

keeping, the *Texas Observer*, the *Los Angeles Times*, and other publications. A former Fulbright scholarship recipient, she was educated at Harvard University, Saint Olaf College, and the University of Texas at Austin, where she was a James A. Michener fellow. She has received awards and recognition for her work from the *Atlantic Monthly*, the Jentel Arts Foundation, the Fine Arts Work Center, the Corporation of Yaddo, and others. She is the recipient of the Philip Roth Writer-in-Residence Fellowship at Bucknell University and the Rona Jaffe Foundation Award for Emerging Women Writers. She currently teaches in the MFA Program at Antioch University–Los Angeles.

Kathy Rhodes is the author of *Pink Butterbeans: Stories from the Heart of a Southern Woman*, a collection of fifty personal essays. She is publisher and editor of the online literary journal *Muscadine Lines: A Southern Journal*, which showcases fiction and creative nonfiction. She currently lives in Franklin, Tennessee, where she serves on the board of directors of the Tennessee Writers Alliance and as president of the Williamson County Council for the Written Word, a nonprofit organization that encourages, educates, and empowers writers. Her blog is called First Draft: Laying Down the Words.

Sean Rowe has been a reporter for the *Miami Herald* and senior writer for the *Miami New Times*. He is the author of *Fever*, a maritime suspense novel published by Little, Brown and Company in 2005. In addition to his career in journalism, Rowe has been employed as a registered nurse on a cancer ward and as a copywriter for North Carolina–based Adam & Eve, "America's Most Trusted Vendor of Adult Products." He is a member of the Authors Guild, the Academy of American Poets, and the North Carolina Writers Network, and serves as a freelance editor for Village Voice Media, LLC.

Dawnelle Wilkie is currently finishing an MFA in Creative Writing at Goddard College. She lives in Washington State with her daughter.

Matt Wood is a writer living in Chicago. His work has appeared in *Anatomy of Baseball*, edited by Lee Gutkind and Andrew Blauner, as well as *Creative Nonfiction*, *Time Out Chicago*, *Elysian Fields Quarterly*, *Chicago Sports Weekly*, and various sites online. He is currently a student in the Northwestern University MFA in Creative Writing program and blogs at wood-tang.com.

Wesley Yang writes for *n+1*, *Nextbook*, and the *Abu Dhabi National*. He has reviewed books for the *New York Times Book Review* and the *Los Angeles Times Book Review*.

where we found
the best creative nonfiction

AGNI, founded in the early 1970s, has always looked to create a cosmopolitan forum for ambitious writing in all fiction, poetry, and nonfiction. "If we favor anything," say the editors, "it's complexity, independence and writing pitched toward lyric precision. Much as we admire hard-bitten realism and far-fringe formal experimentation, we are most open to work that expresses the inner realm with sustained precision and inventive departure. The nonfiction we most prize is ruminative, often but not always memoiristic, and achieves original form as it fulfills the expressive imperative."

The Believer publishes essays, interviews, and book reviews of the highest quality, regardless of length. Written by celebrated contributors such as Zadie Smith, Greil Marcus, Sheila Heti, Rick Moody, and others, *Believer* essays regularly illuminate the singularly entangled world of culture—film, music, books, art, and beyond—while maintaining strong roots in the literary-review tradition. They give new relevance to old topics and works, taking a highbrow approach to pop culture, and a pop approach to highbrow culture.

Bellevue Literary Review is a unique literary magazine that examines human existence through the prism of health and healing, illness and disease. *BLR* publishes two issues a year filled with high-quality, easily accessible poetry, short stories, and essays that appeal to a wide audience of readers. *BLR* seeks perceptive nonfiction that transcends its topic and offers readers insights into the human experience of illness and disease. Its editors say, "We judge creative nonfiction as we would fiction, in terms of character development and specificity of language. We are also looking for literary essays that move beyond the illness narrative format and explore topics more expansively."

Bioethics Forum (www.thehastingscenter.org/BioethicsForum) is an online-only offshoot of the *Hastings Center Report* that has featured diverse, topical commentary on ethical issues in medicine and the life sciences since March 2006. The *Hastings Center Report* is the world's leading periodical engaging ethical issues in health, medicine, and the environment, and how they intersect with public policy. It has published six times a year since 1970 and combines elements of both a scholarly journal and a general-interest literary magazine, including a range of work from peer-reviewed articles to personal narratives. The editors of *Hastings Center Report* and the *Bioethics Forum* look for engaging, accessible writing on interesting ideas. They say, "Everything we publish explores an ethical slant on issues in medicine and the life sciences, but we like to compile a range of work, including scholarly articles in the field, personal narratives, book reviews, and brief opinion pieces."

Cimarron Review has published some of the finest nonfiction, fiction, and poetry, including work by Pulitzer and Nobel Prize winners, from Oklahoma State University since 1967. The editors say, "We admire work that allows us to immediately forget we're reading 'creative nonfiction' and gives us the opportunity to join in someone else's moment. We love writing that is less about pursuing a thesis, and is instead about hanging onto the tale of a runaway story."

Cincinnati Review grew out of the PhD Program in Creative Writing at the University of Cincinnati in 2003. The idea was to create a competitive national journal headed up by a seasoned staff who would take on graduate-student apprentices. These students become well-versed in all aspects of journal publishing over the course of intensive two-year apprenticeships. Say the editors, "We are attracted to nonfiction that presents and explores a slant psychology—albeit as that psychology relates to, and is affected by, external factors and forces."

Gulf Coast strives to publish the best writing from both established and emerging authors. An annual nonfiction prize awards $1,000 and publication for one outstanding piece of nonfiction. The editors say, "While we appreciate a strong narrative essay, we also enjoy publishing nonfiction that takes on less-traditional forms."

Image, a literary and arts quarterly founded in 1989, is a unique forum for writing and artwork that are informed by—or grapple with—religious faith. Each issue explores this relationship through outstanding fiction, poetry, painting, sculpture, architecture, film, music, interviews, and dance. *Image* also features four-color reproductions of visual art. The editors say, "We have never been interested in art that merely regurgitates dogma or falls back on easy answers or didacticism. Instead, our focus has been on writing and visual art that embody a spiritual struggle, that seek to strike a balance between tradition and a profound openness to the world. Here the larger questions of existence intersect with what the poet Albert Goldbarth calls the 'greasy doorknobs and salty tearducts' of our everyday lives."

Isotope: A Journal of Literary Nature and Science Writing explores the worlds of nature and science—from wilderness to astronomy, from urban ecosystems to the body—through stylistically varied literature produced by writers and scientists alike. By wedding an expansive sense of natural history with powerful narratives, memorable images, and striking (even experimental) language, *Isotope*'s poems, essays, and stories appeal to literate readers who seek work that moves beyond traditional nature writing, merely explanatory science journalism, and environmental advocacy. *Isotope* contains fact-based literature that becomes memorable, educational, and moving through the writers' attention to style.

Minnetonka Review is an independent literary journal established in 2006 and published on the shores of Lake Minnetonka, Minnesota. Along with nonfiction, each semi-annual issue features dozens of poems and short stories. About nonfiction the editors say, "We search out writers with strong and original voices who either relate a unique experience or insight, or tell an everyday story in an extraordinary way. The way a story is told can be more intriguing than the story itself. Great writers take chances and defy convention. Our conviction is that successful literary works engage and entertain readers while offering them new perceptions of both themselves and the world at large."

n+1 is a more-or-less twice-yearly magazine of culture, politics, economics, and literature, working especially at the intersection of the four. It believes that most current practices directed toward the preservation of literature lead mostly to the increased isolation of both writing and reading. It has won the Utne Independent Press Award for Best Writing and been widely reviled in the blogosphere. The editors say they seek work for which the author feels there is a pressing necessity because it addresses a contemporary topic in some unique way, or opens another front in the battle for clear, direct, and honest thought.

Oxford American, "the Southern Magazine of Good Writing," is published four times a year from the campus of the University of Central Arkansas. It was founded in 1992 on the grounds that there is room on the newsstands for an ambitious general magazine from the South. Editor and founder Marc Smirnoff says, "I try not to say, in any precise way, what we are looking for because once I do what I'm really hearing is not my voice but the sound of doors shutting. Anyway, if editors could answer with precision about what they are looking for, they wouldn't need writers. Good editors, like good readers, need to be challenged and provoked and invigorated. The writing we seek needs to make us think or feel a little bit differently. This is too much to ask of bad writing; but great writing seems to have a knack for delivering surprises—those little cosmic gifts that we cannot think of, or articulate, for ourselves."

PMS poemmemoirstory is a 140-page, perfect-bound, all-women's literary journal published annually by the University of Alabama at Birmingham. While *PMS* proudly publishes the best work of the best women writers in the nation (for example, Lucille Clifton, Nikki Giovanni, Natasha Trethewey, and Edwidge Danticat), its editors also solicit a memoir for each issue written by a woman who may not be a writer, but who has experienced something of historic significance. Emily Lyons, the nurse who survived the 1998 New Woman All Women Birmingham clinic bombing, wrote the first of these; women who experienced the World Trade Center on September 11, the Civil Rights Movement in Birmingham, the war in Iraq, and Hurricane Katrina have also lent their stories. Founding editor Linda Frost says, "When PMS was launched in 2001, memoirs and works of creative nonfiction were increasingly among the most popular kinds of writing being read around. But what became quickly apparent is how much the form fit what women writers needed and wanted to do—that is, to find a place in a wider linguistic landscape for the stories they needed to tell about themselves. . . . These are words that won't sit still or be quiet on the page; they are undoubtedly the words women have needed to speak for themselves, forever."

The Truth About the Fact: A Journal of Literary Nonfiction is an international journal committed to the idea that excellence in the art of letters can play a vital role in transforming the planet. Says founder Michael Datcher, "We're interested in publishing true stories well told—artful narratives that offer some insight into the human condition while keeping us enraptured during the process of the telling."

Virginia Quarterly Review was founded in 1925 as a journal of "independent thought in the fields of society, politics, and literature," seeking nonfiction from the most original and intelligent writers on a wide range of topics—personal essays, travel writing, historical analysis, political opinion, and criticism. *VQR* opened its pages to all writers who could express daring thoughts in an appealing and arresting way. The current editors say, "We seek essays that show a vital engagement with the world—the world as it is, the world as it might be. We look for writers who are conscious of language without being self-conscious, who pull readers in with drama and emotional risk, rather than holding them at arm's length with gimmickry and tricks. . . . In short, we want our writing to show the craft of literature but the urgency of the day's news."

Witness blends the features of a literary and an issue-oriented magazine to highlight the role of the modern writer as witness to his or her times. Each issue includes fiction, poetry, memoir, and literary essays. The magazine is best known for showcasing work that defines its historical moment; special issues have focused on political oppression, religion, the natural world, crime, aging, civil rights, love, ethnic America, and, most recently, exile.

While the magazine continues to advance topics of special interest, mostly in portfolio form, it increasingly features writing that ventures away from the American experience and into international terrain. The editors say, "*Witness* values the insights of socially aware nonfiction writers who illuminate their circumstances in unique and startling ways. In particular, we look for essays and memoir that expand our knowledge of contemporary events and places beyond an author's firsthand experience of them. We welcome formally inventive and more traditional narrative styles, alike."

credits

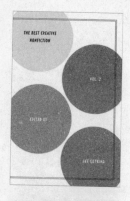

The Best Creative Nonfiction Vols. 1 & 2

Creative nonfiction at its cutting-edge best. Lee Gutkind has scoured alternative publications, blogs, literary journals, and other often-overlooked publications in search of new voices and innovative ideas for essays.

> "The richness of the 'real' makes the anthology work as a cohesive whole."
> —*Publishers Weekly*

Keep It Real

All the necessary tools to write nonfiction, whether you're starting out or have been writing for years.

> "Largely practical and eminently helpful, *Keep It Real* is the perfect book for those taking their first tentative steps into this versatile and (relatively) brave new world."
> —Michael G. Cornelius,
> *The Bloomsbury Review*

In Fact

This collection, a decade of the best works from the journal *Creative Nonfiction*, gives a cross section of the famous and those bound to become so, highlighting the expanding importance of this exciting new genre. Contributors include Annie Dillard, John McPhee, and John Edgar Wideman.